What leaders are saying

Scott Wilson has written many good books on leadership, but this one is different. This book is about the art of pastoral leadership, specifically, how to lead God's people in hearing His voice. In these pages, Scott lays out a clear process for engaging your church in being truly Pentecostal, activating the gifts of the Spirit, and allowing the Spirit to speak to and through every Spirit-filled believer. Read this prayerfully, step out and practice it yourself, and lead your people in it. The book you're about to read could change everything for you and your church!

John Davidson, Ph.D.
Director of the Alliance for AG Higher Education,
Director of CMN Leadership Development, AG National
Office, Springfield, Missouri

Powerful, Practical, Enlightening, Inspiring . . . As Pastor Scott Wilson unpacks the richness of 1 Corinthians 12-14, he opens up our minds to embrace all God desires for us as believers. And as the church begins to practice this kind of praying, it is sure to revolutionize every participant and empower the church to walk in God's presence and power as never before. Don't miss this powerful book!

Micheal Dickenson
Network Pastor, New Mexico Ministry Network, Albuquerque,
New Mexico

I am so excited for the leaders of my church to be able to read this book! P3 was such a compelling read as Pastor Scott breaks down 1 Corinthians 12-14. It is written in a practical way that makes applying these truths obtainable for any believer. I have had the honor of seeing the principles of this book lived out in real life through Pastor Scott and the staff at Oaks Church, and I am thrilled that he has written P3 so that many others can experience the precise direction of the Spirit in their churches!

Michael S. Carlton
Lead Pastor, Bloom Church, Branson, Missouri

Many people, even many church leaders, have trouble discerning the heart and will of God. In P3, Scott Wilson explains how God has led him in a process of discovery as he studied Paul's first letter to the Corinthians. Pastor Scott has clearly articulated the difference the Holy Spirit makes in the lives of believers and in the church, and he shares the process he uses with teams as they pray in the Spirit, trust God for understanding of what they've prayed, and agree together that they've accurately heard God's voice. This is a process all of us can use . . . and it's a process our people and our churches desperately need!

Chris Railey
Sr. Director Leadership/Church Development, The General Council of the Assemblies of God, Springfield, Missouri

I am impressed with the simplicity of a powerful truth Scott Wilson so thoroughly unfolds in his book, *P3*. I have been a Spirit-filled believer since childhood and learned long ago the value of praying in the Spirit; however, I have fallen short of considering the spiritual rhythm Scott describes as praying in the Spirit, then getting the understanding of what you have prayed, and finally, praying in agreement with what the Spirit is saying. It's a rhythm for life and needs to be internalized by every leader, pastor, and child of God in our movement. One of the results of practicing P3 is unity in the body of Christ. "It's there that the Lord bestows His blessing, even life forevermore!" I desire the Lord's blessing. I want those I lead to share in His blessing. Pastor Scott unfolds a critical truth that the modern-day Spirit-filled church needs today.

Pastor Stephen Harris
Superintendent, Arizona Ministry Network, Phoenix, Arizona

Our ministry team has had the privilege of hearing Scott Wilson speak on several occasions. We have been blessed by his ability to lead through the moving of the Spirit. His understanding of the way individual gifts operate in a corporate setting is truly anointed. In *P3* Scott helps all leaders interpret how we pray in the Spirit with prophetic understanding. He shows how a group of people can all hear the same message from God. A recommended read for *all church leaders*.

Franklin H. Potter
Superintendent, Potomac Ministry Network, Gainesville, Virginia

We were privileged to have Pastor Scott Wilson introduce the P3 prayer model at our Ministers Retreat. We experienced a corporate anointing as we prayed in the Spirit, and the Holy Spirit opened up our understanding of what He wants to do in Indiana. We have practiced this model with our pastors-in-training and our Executive and Ministry Group Presbyters. Each time, we received divine revelation and encouragement. One of the elements I appreciate about this prayer model is the quiet time when we listen. Being quiet and listening is a great practice for Pentecostal leaders. I love the collective prophetic words that come as each person shares what the Holy Spirit is saying so we can all walk in agreement with each other. Jesus is our great intercessor, and we are learning to pray what Jesus prays and the Holy Spirit prays through us.

Pastor Don Gifford
Superintendent of the Indiana District of the Assemblies of God,
Indianapolis, Indiana

Do you have a longing to move forward in powerful prayer and prophetic and revelatory experiences in pursuit of God's will together with your people? *P3* just might provide a strong pathway for you to do so. This book covers the biblical foundations for this process and presents practical approaches for leaders at every level of God's work.

Paul Brooks, D.Min.
Professor of Theology and Vice President for Academics at
Southwestern Assemblies of God University, Waxahachie, Texas

The P3 prayer model is transformative. When I first saw it practiced I thought, "This is part of what I've been looking for in the last twenty years of ministry—a renewed way forward for the Spirit-empowered church that's both alive with spiritual gifts and yet steps away from some of the baggage of past expressions." We use it weekly in our church and with our staff! It's theologically rich, spiritually alive, and practically simple to implement.

Dr. Douglas Witherup
Lead Pastor of cfa Church and author of Interrobang
Preaching

Millennials love the supernatural and are open to deep and personal encounters with God's Spirit. Pastor Scott, with clarity, experience and passion, unveils a dimension of communication with the Divine in an accessible way for everyone.

Dr. Michael Rakes
Senior Pastor of WSFirst in Winston Salem, North Carolina,
author of Slings and Stones

P3 is truly God inspired. Pastor Wilson has listened to the call of God to provide us with a way to lift and encourage His people through the Holy Spirit. This book teaches us how to hear and share God's word for the people around us. I can truly say that the P3 system is a gift from God to the Body of Christ. Thank you, Pastor Scott, for sharing this teaching with us. Our congregation has been blessed by you.

Dr. Lee Scott, D.D
Bishop of Lively Stone Church, St. Louis, Missouri

God's prophetic direction is so amazing, so wise, and so deep that at times it has been misinterpreted. Many pastors have stories about the problems they have experienced with people and prophecies. That is why *P3* is so important for the church, staff and individuals: it brings clarity about what God is speaking into their lives and the direction that God is leading them. One of the most powerful points in Pastor Scott's book is that the process doesn't focus on an individual's ability to hear from God, but instead, it involves the Body of Christ. In this way, it unites people and provides clarity about what God is speaking. God has given Pastor Scott an amazing revelation in *P3*. I believe it will help pastors and church leaders be more confident in their prophetic ministry and embrace the prophetic in a more sound, balanced and powerful way. I have been blessed by *P3*, and I recommend it to every pastor.

Richard Martinez
Lead Pastor of Iglesia CAFE (CAFE Church), Arlington, Texas

SCOTT WILSON

Praying . . .
in the Spirit,
with understanding, and
in agreement

ISBN: 978-1-951022-00-6
Cover design and interior formatting by Anne McLaughlin,
Blue Lake Design
Published by Oaks Resources
Printed in the United States

I dedicate this book to the people of Oaks Church.
You are the most gracious and wonderful
people in the world.
I'm honored to be your Pastor.

CONTENTS

THIS CHANGES EVERYTHING!

In the last several years at our church, God has opened our hearts and minds to a different level of interacting with Him in prayer. We are praying in the Spirit with great power and listening for God to give us revelation . . . and He does. We're learning to listen as a team and in every aspect of church life, as well as individually. The Spirit isn't just moving every now and then; He's manifesting himself to us regularly, and it has become a new normal—a thrilling new normal! These experiences are transforming our lives, our teams, and everyone at Oaks Church. It's AMAZING, but I wonder why I didn't see this before.

When I was eight years old, our family went to a camp meeting—yes, a camp meeting . . . in a tent. At the end of one of the services, the pastor gave his invitation: "If any of you want to experience more of God, come up and we'll pray for you." As people went forward, the rest of the crowd started singing a hymn.

I turned to my father and whispered, "Dad, you always pray in the Spirit, and there's always something powerful about it. I wish I could pray like you do. Would you go down front with me and ask God to help me to pray that way?" Whenever I was upset as a little boy, my father took me in his arms and prayed in the Spirit. It meant so much to me, and I wanted what he had.

We walked forward together. At the makeshift altar, he told me, "Son, it's a gift, and you can receive it. When He gives it, just speak it out."

After about five minutes, words I'd never known began coming out of my mouth. It was the first time I spoke in tongues. I cried with joy, and Dad was thrilled.

When we went back to the place where we'd been sitting, Dad leaned over and said, "Now son, if you don't use it, you're going to lose it." He wasn't warning me that I'd actually lose the gift, but he was encouraging me to let my prayer language be a regular part of my walk with God.

I prayed in the Spirit for the rest of my childhood, into my twenties when I responded to God's call to be a pastor, into my thirties when I was running hard after God, and now in my forties when God began to give me more insight about the beauty and power of this gift. During all these years, I felt connected with God and deeply encouraged when I prayed in the Spirit. But only a few years ago as I read 1 Corinthians 14, I saw something I'd never noticed before. Paul explained,

> For this reason the one who speaks in a tongue should pray that they may interpret what they say. For if I pray in a tongue, my spirit prays, but my mind is unfruitful. So what shall I do? I will pray with my spirit, but I will also pray with my understanding; I will sing with my spirit, but I will also sing with my understanding. (1 Corinthians 14:13–15)

I will pray . . . with understanding. I will sing . . . with understanding. I was 40 years old, and I'd taught the Scriptures (and this passage!) many times, but I'd never noticed that Paul said the gift of tongues can be and should be accompanied with under-standing. While we know that Paul's primary purpose in writing 1 Corinthians 12-14 is to help establish godly order in the con-gregation, these passages also outline basic concepts of how the Spirit manifests himself, sometimes in corporate settings, some-times in one-on-one encounters, and sometimes in private.

Before this moment, I thought tongues served to bring a gen-eral feeling of encouragement and being close to God—which, to be honest, is pretty magnificent! And I engaged the gift more when I felt burdened and wanted God to lead me, but I never assumed God would give me an interpretation of tongues as I prayed individually. As I sat with my Bible open and stared at this passage, I sensed God say, "I'd like to let you know what I'm pray-ing through you."

With the realization that a huge door had opened to God, I sat back and said, "This changes everything!"

I want to tell you the story of how God has led me, our team, and our church into this revelation, then we'll look at the biblical foundation, the practical process of how we do it, and finally, how to pastor the process. I hope it changes everything for you too.

CHAPTER 1

TWO EYES, TWO EARS

From the day God showed me what the passage in 1 Corinthians was really saying, I took time to reflect on the thoughts that came to mind as I prayed in the Spirit. Quite often, I had a very clear sense that God was giving me an interpretation of my prayer. Like any skill, getting the interpretations right takes practice, and I'm sure I got some things wrong. But there were plenty of times when it was obvious that God was giving me His mind, His heart, and His direction.

My new insights and experiences in prayer were so powerful that soon I told my staff team what God was teaching me, and I encouraged them to ask God for an interpretation as they prayed in the Spirit. They took time to consider what came to mind as they prayed, and God began to reveal himself to them as well. We were praying in the Spirit and with understanding individually, and when we came together, we shared what God had been praying though each of us, or in some cases, we shared the prophetic word God had spoken back to us by His Spirit. It was electric!

As my faith grew, more passages leaped off the pages of the Bible. Earlier in Paul's first letter to the Corinthians, he assures them that the message he has proclaimed to them is categorically different than the message of the world's authorities:

> My message and my preaching were not with wise and persuasive words, but with a demonstration of the Spirit's power, so that your faith might not rest on human wisdom, but on God's power. We do, however, speak a message of wisdom among the mature, but not the wisdom of this age or of the rulers of this age, who are coming to nothing. No, we declare God's wisdom, a mystery that has been hidden and that God destined for our glory before time began. None of the rulers of this age understood it, for if they had, they would not have crucified the Lord of glory. However, as it is written:
>
> "What no eye has seen,
>   what no ear has heard,
>   and what no human mind has conceived"—
>   the things God has prepared for those who love
>   him—
>
> these are the things God has revealed to us by his Spirit. ... The person with the Spirit makes judgments about all things, but such a person is not subject to merely human judgments, for,
>
> "Who has known the mind of the Lord
>   so as to instruct him?"
>   But we have the mind of Christ.
>   (1 Corinthians 2:4–10, 15–16)

I began to believe that God is more interested in giving us His insights and instructions than keeping them hidden as a mystery. I finally understood what it means to "have the mind of Christ"! The people on our team had the same renewed faith. We experienced God's presence, power, and leading more than ever . . . because we understood that God wanted to give us His interpretation as we prayed in the Spirit.

We experienced God's presence, power, and leading more than ever . . . because we understood that God wanted to give us His interpretation as we prayed in the Spirit.

After a few weeks, one of our staff members said, "Can we do this together and see what God says to us?"

I instantly replied, "Of course! Let's pray together in the Spirit and then with understanding. Each of us should expect to receive something from God after praying in the Spirit. He'll either give us the interpretation of what our spirits are praying, or He'll give us a vision, a word of wisdom or knowledge, or a prophetic word in response to our Spirit-inspired prayers."

I wanted to back up and explain things from the beginning. I told them the story about asking my Dad to pray that God would enable me to pray in the Spirit, and I explained that praying in tongues had been encouraging to me for many years. The passage I'd pointed to all my life was 1 Corinthians 14:4: "Anyone who speaks in a tongue edifies himself." There's nothing wrong with that! But there's more: We looked again at the passage in 1 Corinthians 14:13–15 and talked about connecting interpretation with praying in the Spirit. We looked at the passage that says we can pray with understanding and sing with understanding. We also looked at a passage in Romans: "In the same way, the Spirit helps us in our weakness. We do not know what we ought to pray for, but the Spirit himself intercedes for us through wordless groans. And he who searches our hearts knows the mind of the Spirit, because the Spirit intercedes for God's people in accordance with the will of God" (Romans 8:26–27).

I asked our team, "Do we want to understand what God is praying through us?" I didn't wait for an answer. "Of course we do."

Then I told them, "Okay, let's do it. Take some time to pray in the Spirit." After a few minutes, we stopped praying, and I said, "Let's ask God for understanding." I prayed, "God, Paul was inspired by Your Spirit when he wrote that when we pray in the Spirit we can get understanding, and that's what we ask You for right now. Please give us understanding of what we've been praying. We receive it now in Jesus' name."

I gave them a minute or two to hear from God. As I watched them, they were intent, but many of them were smiling. After a few minutes, I asked, "So, what understanding is God giving you? Did you get an interpretation of your Spirit prayer, or a prophetic vision or word in response? You don't have to tell us if it's too personal, but we'd love to hear it."

People talked about God's heart for the people in our church and our community, His encouragement that we were on the right track, His desire that we honor Him in other countries, and the fruit that God was going to bring as we follow Him. Some of the comments were global, but others were very specific. We were sure that God was among us and revealing His heart to us.

When we got together for our next staff meeting, everyone knew what was first on the agenda. Almost in unison, people said, "Let's do it again!" Nobody wondered what "it" was. Again, we prayed in the Spirit and asked God for understanding, and again, it was a powerful experience.

After about a month or so of praying, listening, and sharing together, I thought, *What if we ask God to give us understanding about a specific issue we're facing as a team?* This wasn't exactly "out of the blue." We needed to raise $18 million for our new building, and we needed God to provide.

Yeah, I know what you're thinking. I admit that I was really slow to connect this kind of prayer with specific needs, but God was taking me where I'd never been before, so slow was just fine with me.

Raising that much money was weighing heavy on me. But actually, the amount of money wasn't the issue. I've been burdened every time our church has grown and we needed to build more space, so the pressure was nothing new. I had some pressing questions: How much could we raise? How much would we need to borrow? Would the bank loan us this much? Should we even build this new building at all, or is this something that's not in God's plan? They were familiar questions, but this time, I had a new resource. I told the team about my concerns, and I asked, "We need to hear from God about all this. Will you pray with me?" They all agreed to pray with me about the problem, and one of them assured me, "God will give us an answer." And He did. God gave each of us a piece of the answer: Yes, He was going to provide, but there would be some surprises along the way. In each step, we could trust God's sovereignty and goodness. He was going to honor himself throughout the process. At the end of our prayer and sharing, I was tremendously relieved.

Our perspective on prayer had evolved and now was very different than before. Prayer no longer *opened* the agenda; prayer *set* our agenda. As we listened to the Spirit give us understanding of our prayers, we became more sensitive to the voice of God. Sometimes God led us to pray for a particular person or a specific need, but at other times we asked God to give us wisdom about our direction, a ministry, an outreach, or another big issue. Nothing was off limits, and God met us each time.

I'm on a team of national leaders to plant churches in every community in the United States. God is using the Church Multiplication Network in incredible ways. Over the span of three recent years, over 1100 churches were planted. The leadership team meets twice a year. A year and a half after the adventure of prayer began, I attended one of our meetings in Washington, D.C., at Mark Batterson's church. Chris Railey, the Director of CMN, texted me the night before the first meeting and asked me to lead a devotional the next day. He asked me to share what I'd learned about praying in the Spirit and with understanding, and then we could pray and ask God for direction as an organization. Chris had been on staff with us at Oaks Church before becoming the Director of CMN, so he was aware of all that had happened on our team.

The next morning, I told the group of about a dozen people the story of how God had given me insight into the 1 Corinthians 14 passage and how He had been leading our team to pray in the Spirit and trust Him for understanding. I shared a couple of stories, and then I said, "I think it would be great if we pray in the Spirit and then ask God to reveal His heart to us. He may give us the interpretation of what we were praying in the Spirit, or He may give us prophetic insight, a word of knowledge or wisdom concerning this ministry."

At that moment, Mark Batterson leaned back in his chair. He looked deep in thought. I had wondered if he was going to shoot holes in my ideas from the beginning. After a few seconds he said, "Wow. We need to pay close attention to this. I remember when I was at my father-in-law's church years ago. Every time there were prophetic words in the services, Pastor Schmidgall wrote them down. The next day, he asked his administrative assistant to type them and compile them in the church's files. For each year he pastored the church, he had a file of all the prophetic words spoken in the worship services. He often pulled out the files to look at how God had spoken to the church, and he looked for patterns to discern the movement of the Spirit over time."

At that moment, God brought 1 Peter 4:11 to mind: "If anyone speaks, they should do so as one who speaks the very words of God." It hit me: the understanding God gives us as we pray constitutes "the very words of God." This isn't on the same level as Scripture, but it's His word given for His glory to meet the needs of His children. It's God's message for that house and that moment, and if God is speaking to us, like Mark said, we should pay attention to it.

We took some time to pray in the Spirit, and then I invited them, "When you sense God revealing something to you, go ahead and share it." A couple of people had images come to mind, a few said God put particular passages of Scripture on their hearts, and they shared them, and some people had a word or a phrase.

As each person spoke, God was giving us clear direction, encouragement, and the challenge to take His hand and follow Him wherever He leads. God was going to open doors for us, and He was going to do some magnificent things. Some of us were crying, and some were almost laughing. After everyone shared, we all sat back and marveled at what God had spoken to and through each of us. It was awesome.

As each person spoke, God was giving us clear direction, encouragement, and the challenge to take His hand and follow Him wherever He leads.

Later that day, I thought long and hard about Mark's comments about Pastor Schmidgall recording every prophetic word in his church. I planned to do the same thing and see if they create a pattern of God's leading at The Oaks.

When I got home, I told our staff about the amazing prayer meeting with the CMN leadership team, and I said, "Now, when we pray and share, I'm going to write down the revelation God gives to us, whether it's an interpretation of what He's praying through us or a prophetic word in response to our prayers. I want to know if there's a pattern we need to pay attention to."

We prayed in the Spirit, and then I asked them to share what God had revealed to them. I wrote down what each one said, and when we were finished, I read them all back to the team. We were stunned. Someone said, "It sounds like each of us had one piece of a puzzle . . . or one sentence in a story. They all fit together into one message! God is revealing His heart to us!"

I thought about the cards people are given at the Super Bowl, the Olympics, and a few other major sporting events. Everyone has one card with one color, and when the signal is given, they hold them up. In the stands, they can't see the image made by the tens of thousands of cards, but from the blimp (or the bleachers), the message is crystal clear. That's a picture of what had happened in our staff meeting!

Actually, I thought it was a one-time event. It was wonderful, but I had no idea it could happen again. The next week, we did it again, and the same thing happened: God gave each of us a piece of the fabric of His love and leading. It happened again and again. At this point, what we now commonly call "P3" took shape: we were praying in the Spirit, with understanding, and in agreement.

I decided to introduce the concepts and practices to our board and elders. I walked them through the story of how our staff team had come to this point, and I invited them to pray in the Spirit and trust God for understanding. A few of them were a bit reluctant. They didn't want to be the only one who didn't hear from God! But soon, they relaxed and were open to let God pray through them and listen for the understanding. They were also open to the fact that they might pray in the Spirit and receive a prophetic word or vision, but if they didn't, that was fine too. There is, I explained, no pressure to make anything happen. The metaphor of the cards in stadiums made sense to them, and I explained, "God will only give you one card. If you get it, hold it up. It doesn't have to make sense by itself, but with the other cards, it'll form a powerful picture."

I noticed that in almost every group, people flow in gifts other than just tongues and interpretation of tongues. Paul makes it clear in 1 Corinthians 14 that the gift of tongues is expressed in four ways: mysteries, prayer, praise, and thanksgiving—all directed toward God. It follows, then, that the interpretation of tongues is similarly directed toward God.[1] In tongues, our spirit is praying to God in alignment with the Holy Spirit, bypassing our minds. And when we get an interpretation, God is giving us the ability to pray His prayers along with Him. But often as we P3, God chooses to respond to our prayers with gifts of prophecy, words of knowledge, and words of wisdom. In most cases that we've experienced, people either see visions, get a Scripture, or have a word or phrase come to mind. Some people see images that sometimes need their own interpretations, others typically say that God put a passage from the Bible on their hearts, and still others have a single word, such as "peace" or a phrase or a sentence, such as, "God is saying, 'I'm your Father. You can trust Me.'" God still speaks in many different ways, and we have the incredible privilege of listening to Him.

We've always said our church is a Spirit-led organization, but now we really are. We no longer go to God with our best guess at what He wants, and we don't ask Him to bless our personal agenda; we expect God to set our agenda. And I'm not "the answer man." I'm the leader who sets the environment for God to speak to all of us, not just me. Through our team, God gives wisdom, affirmation, and direction.

---

1   For more about the God-focused nature of tongues and interpretation, see "P3: A Biblical Perspective" by Dr. John Davidson in the appendix of this book.

I've learned to pastor the process. For instance, when someone says simply "peace," I ask God if there's more to it, and He may remind me of the passage like the one in Philippians where Paul tells them, "Do not be anxious about anything, but in every situation, by prayer and petition, with thanksgiving, present your requests to God. And the peace of God, which transcends all understanding, will guard your hearts and your minds in Christ Jesus" (Philippians 4:6–7).

A few months after I got back from the CMN leadership meetings, I realized that I needed to give members of our church staff the opportunity to lead the team in prayer and understanding. It was a safe and encouraging spiritual laboratory, and over time all of us learned to be more skilled in leading this kind of P3 prayer. They all now use this method in meetings with their teams: children, youth, small groups, missions, worship, administration, facilities, and all the rest. P3 is now an integral part of the culture of The Oaks.

Obviously, learning to tap into the heart and mind of God has revolutionized my life, our team, and the ministry of our church. Let me outline a few ways it has made a difference:

- It has taken a huge load off my shoulders. I used to believe that I was the only one with the responsibility to hear from God and give direction to the church, but now God speaks through our team. It's still my role to lead them, but God speaks to each of us. As a leader, I can relax much more because my team is highly motivated to do all God says to them.

- God uses our team to pick me up when I'm struggling. Sometimes, I'll tell them I'm worried about something, and they hear from God and tell me what He's saying. Other times, I don't tell them what's going on with me, but as we pray and listen, God gives them a word of encouragement that applies specifically to me and my situation. Similarly, when I've felt confused as I've prayed on my own about a difficult circumstance, I've asked our team to pray, and God has given very clear direction. This has given me more peace, joy, and confidence than you can imagine. Now, as our team prays about the church's future, I'm sure that God is guiding us!

- I don't have to manipulate or pressure people to do what God wants them to do. There's one head to this body, and it's not me! All of us can hear from God, so all of us get excited to put our piece of the puzzle with the others. The difference between manipulation and motivation is clear: manipulation is when we try to force (by intimidation or more subtle means) to get people to accomplish our agenda, but motivation is encouraging them to do what they know God wants them to do. My role is never to manipulate, and when people hear from God, I do more cheerleading and guiding because they're already motivated.

- Team relationships are much stronger and deeper because it's no longer (or very seldom) "my will" against "your will." It's always about God's will. P3 is a unifying power on our team. There's much less competition to prove we're smarter or more spiritual than someone else, and there's much more compassion and encouragement. I never sense that anyone is trying to one-up the rest of us with a more powerful word from God as we P3. I'm not saying it can't happen, but in my experience, the sense of humility and privilege overcomes the insecurity that's the source of unhealthy competition. We have a powerful sense that our time of prayer and listening is far bigger than ourselves, and it's an honor to play a small part.

- As P3 has filtered into every corner of our church, we're seeing a lot of people learning to pray in the Spirit with understanding. Everyone can exercise the gift of tongues and trust God for understanding and revelation. Is this a threat to my leadership? Not in the least. When God raised up two men to prophesy to the children of Israel, Joshua was angry and tried to stop them, but Moses told him, "Are you jealous for my sake? I wish that all the LORD's people were prophets and that the LORD would put his Spirit on them!" (Numbers 11:29) Like Moses, I wish that all God's people would receive prophetic words in prayer and share them with others.

- As more people are praying in the Spirit, with understanding, and in agreement, they're taking more responsibility for the life of the church. When they hear about a need, they don't immediately assume they can't handle it and call the church office. They pray in the Spirit and with understanding on their own. They gather in their small group or with friends and pray so they can hear from God. In this way, ministry is decentralized as many people are hearing from God and holding up their cards in the stadium. I don't have to be the only person praying Spirit-empowered prayers and getting a word from God. My role is still crucial, but now I'm one of many who know how to P3 and get direction from the Lord.

- As more teams, small groups, and ministries practice P3, there's a growing undercurrent of excitement and expectation.

People who are entrepreneurial are learning to trust God to speak through a group of people, not only to one leader. And those who are temperamentally cautious, even resistant, are becoming more optimistic as they see God affirm a direction for their team. Hearing from God gives direction, affirms that direction, and convinces people that God is in the middle of their calling and work. Early adopters jump on board quickly, but we're seeing middle and late adopters move much more quickly and be far more positive than before because they understand that their "card" is an important part of the whole picture, and they were in the room when God spoke through each person! When people realize they're hearing from God instead of just a person, their fear subsides, their excitement builds, and they can't wait to dive into the tasks of ministry to see God's leading become a reality.

Today, about a tenth of the people in our church can lead a P3 time of prayer. Of course, many more have participated in these experiences, and it's thrilling to see so many people take the lead in tapping into God's mind and heart.

At the end of each chapter, you'll find some questions designed to help you and your team reflect on the concepts of P3 and apply them. Don't hurry through them. Take your time, read, think, pray, and trust God to speak to you as you consider them.

Think about it:

1. Read 1 Corinthians 14:13–15. How have you understood this passage before reading about "understanding" in the opening section called "This Changes Everything!"? How do you understand it now?

2. Does the idea of praying in the Spirit, with understanding, and in agreement sound odd to you, or does it sound good, right, and exciting? Explain your answer.

3. Which of the benefits described in this chapter are most attractive to you? How would it (or they) change your life and ministry?

LOUDER, CLEARER

The principles and practices of P3 started when the scales fell off my eyes and God revealed to me the deeper truth found in 1 Corinthians 14 about praying in the Spirit and with understanding. I immediately wondered why I'd never seen this before—and I wondered if I was only seeing what I wanted to see. Was I doing *exegesis*, letting the Scriptures speak through accurate observation, interpretation, and application, or was this only *eisegesis*, proof texting and reading my opinions into the text? Was this something that meets the test of rigorous biblical analysis, or was it only my desire for something fresh and new? These weren't questions I answered quickly. I wanted to sit with them, hold the concepts up to the light of the whole counsel of God, and invite wise and godly people to give me feedback.

Not on Our Own

I started with the Great Commission. Jesus told the disciples to go and make disciples in all nations, but before they would go, they needed the vital resource of God's Spirit to empower them.

Before Jesus ascended to the Father, He told them, "Do not leave Jerusalem, but wait for the gift my Father promised, which you have heard me speak about. For John baptized with water, but in a few days you will be baptized with the Holy Spirit" (Acts 1:4–5). I can imagine a confused look on their faces, so Jesus explained, "But you will receive power when the Holy Spirit comes on you; and you will be my witnesses in Jerusalem, and in all Judea and Samaria, and to the ends of the earth" (Acts 1:8).

Jesus gave them the greatest task the world has ever known, but they couldn't accomplish it on their own. They needed the Holy Spirit's presence and power. Ten days later, as they were in the upper room, the Holy Spirit came upon them: "Suddenly a sound like the blowing of a violent wind came from heaven and filled the whole house where they were sitting. They saw what seemed to be tongues of fire that separated and came to rest on each of them. All of them were filled with the Holy Spirit and began to speak in other tongues as the Spirit enabled them" (Acts 2:2–4).

Pilgrims from all over the Roman world were at the Feast of Pentecost that day, and they heard the disciples speaking the wonders of God in their own languages. They didn't need an interpretation; in fact, they didn't even need a translation. Many of those listening were confused, and some assumed the disciples were drunk! Peter stood up and pastored the moment:

> Then Peter stood up with the Eleven, raised his voice and addressed the crowd: "Fellow Jews and all of you who live in Jerusalem, let me explain this to you; listen carefully to what I say. These people are not drunk, as you suppose. It's only nine in the morning! No, this is what was spoken by the prophet Joel:

'In the last days, God says,
    I will pour out my Spirit on all people.
Your sons and daughters will prophesy,
    your young men will see visions,
    your old men will dream dreams.
Even on my servants, both men and women,
    I will pour out my Spirit in those days,
    and they will prophesy.
I will show wonders in the heavens above
    and signs on the earth below,
    blood and fire and billows of smoke.
The sun will be turned to darkness
    and the moon to blood
    before the coming of the great and glorious day of the
Lord.
And everyone who calls
    on the name of the Lord will be saved.'" (Acts 2:14–21)

The Spirit was being poured out on "all people," not just a few: sons and daughters, young and old, servants and leaders—and they will prophesy, see visions, and dream dreams. The "last days" started at Pentecost and continues until Jesus returns to make all things right. In this part of the last days, God's people will prophesy, and in the latter part, signs of natural wonders will tell people that Jesus' return is near. Notice that Peter wasn't telling them that everything is brand new. He's saying that what they were seeing had been foretold centuries before by the prophet Joel. They were witnessing the fulfillment of God's plan motivated by God's heart of love for all people.

Praying in the Spirit

Years later, Paul explained that God gives believers the ability to "speak in the tongues of men or of angels" (1 Corinthians 13:1). Paul goes on to explain: "For anyone who speaks in a tongue does not speak to people but to God. Indeed, no one understands them; they utter mysteries by the Spirit" (1 Corinthians 14:2). Paul didn't mean these were "mysteries" in the sense of something spooky or dark, but in the sense that these tongues are understood through the Holy Spirit and not by natural processes. Earlier in the letter to the Christians in Corinth, Paul needed to identify the source of God's wisdom: "What we have received is not the spirit of the world, but the Spirit who is from God, so that we may understand what God has freely given us. This is what we speak, not in words taught us by human wisdom but in words taught by the Spirit, explaining spiritual realities with Spirit-taught words" (1 Corinthians 2:12–13).

In Romans, Paul assures us that the Spirit himself is praying in us and through us: "In the same way, the Spirit helps us in our weakness. We do not know what we ought to pray for, but the Spirit himself intercedes for us through wordless groans. And he who searches our hearts knows the mind of the Spirit, because the Spirit intercedes for God's people in accordance with the will of God" (Romans 8:26–27). I understand this to mean that when we pray in tongues, the Holy Spirit is praying through us, and because our prayers are united with His, we're praying according to God's will without any interference caused by our souls—which is our flawed and limited understanding, our fears and often misplaced hopes, and our intentions that always fall short of God's perfect will.

That's why Paul says, "Anyone who speaks in a tongue edifies himself." How would it not build a person up in faith to pray in concert with the Spirit's heart, love, and will? I realized I'd been thinking about the gift of tongues in a very shallow way. I'd seen it as a "prayer filler," but I began to see it as aligning my heart with God's heart and my prayers with the Spirit's prayers.

> *I'd seen it as a "prayer filler," but I began to see it as aligning my heart with God's heart and my prayers with the Spirit's prayers.*

With Understanding

I often go back to the beginning: God has called me to participate in His grand plan to take the gospel of grace to every person in every corner of the world, but I'm totally inadequate. I desperately need God's intervention to give me direction, power, and love for the people He wants us to reach. The gift of tongues is divine communication, and God wants me to pray "with understanding" so I'm less confused and more in tune with His plans. My confidence isn't based on my ability; it's based on God's promise to connect my prayers with His will. In his first letter, John assures us, "This is the confidence we have in approaching God: that if we ask anything according to his will, he hears us. And if we know that he hears us—whatever we ask—we know that we have what we asked of him" (1 John 5:14–15). If my prayer language is connected with the very heart and will of God, I can have confidence that He hears and He will answer. I don't want to just pray *to* God . . . I want to pray *with* God!

So now, when I pray in tongues, I ask God for understanding. This isn't presumptuous at all. God *wants* us to understand. He *longs* to reveal His will to us, for us to understand what He's praying through us so that we experience more of His power, His leading, and the warmth of His love. As this happens, resistance is eroded, and increasingly, joyful submission is the only reasonable choice. More than ever, I want to be in alignment with God, which is encouraged when I pray in the Spirit and trust Him for understanding.

In Agreement

The third component is crucial. We pray in the Spirit, we pray expecting God to give us understanding, and we pray in agreement as God reveals His will to us through interpretation, words of wisdom and knowledge, and prophetic words. We live in an age of rampant individualism, and the church has been deeply affected by this cultural perspective that we don't really need community to thrive. And it's not just "those people." A lot of Christians assume they can walk with God without being involved in deep, iron-sharpening-iron relationships with other believers. In this section of Paul's first letter to the Corinthians, he dispels that false assumption. In Chapter 12, he says that every Christian has been divinely equipped by God with a spiritual gifts "for the common good," not just for our pleasure or to inflate our reputations. He then goes to great lengths to explain that we're part of a body with Jesus as the head, and all the parts are crucial for the body to function properly. There are no second-class people in God's kingdom.

In Chapter 13, he says that the function of our gifts, our leadership, and our dedication mean nothing if we're not motivated by love. He summarizes his point: "Love never fails. But where there are prophecies, they will cease; where there are tongues, they will be stilled; where there is knowledge, it will pass away. For we know in part and we prophesy in part, but when completeness comes, what is in part disappears" (1 Corinthians 13:8–10). When Jesus returns and we're with Him in the restored Eden of the new heavens and new earth, we won't need tongues, words of knowledge, or prophecy because we'll be face to face with Jesus. In the meantime, though, all these gifts are given "in part." I believe this means that each of us in the body plays a part, but none of us has the whole picture. As we live and serve together, God gives us a more complete picture of His glory, His will, and His heart. Will we get it all here? No, not until we're glorified and forever changed.

As we live and serve together, God gives us a more complete picture of His glory, His will, and His heart.

In Chapter 14, Paul specifically addresses the expression of the gifts of tongues, interpretation, and prophecy. I'm afraid most people who go to church arrive with the goal of receiving something from God, from the pastor, or from the person sitting nearby. But Paul says that we gather to give instead of only receiving: "When you come together, each of you has a hymn, or a word of instruction, a revelation, a tongue or an interpretation. Everything must be done so that the church may be built up" (1 Corinthians 14:26). He then gives detailed instructions:

> Two or three prophets should speak, and the others should weigh carefully what is said. And if a revelation comes to someone who is sitting down, the first speaker should stop. For you can all prophesy in turn so that everyone may be instructed and encouraged. The spirits of prophets are subject to the control of prophets. For God is not a God of disorder but of peace—as in all the congregations of the Lord's people. (1 Corinthians 14:29–33)

For many years, I had no idea what it meant for "the first speaker" to "stop." As our staff team, board and elders practiced P3, I realized that everyone stops because no one has the whole message from God. Each of us stops and welcomes others to share what God has said to them. In this way, we "all prophesy in turn." Each one has a piece, one card to hold up, and together, they form the whole. When everyone understands their role, much of the weirdness vanishes because no one is expected to have the complete, definitive word from God, so no one dominates the others.

In a group of people practicing P3, each person is responsible to play a key part, but of course, each one can hinder or grieve the Spirit instead of flowing with the Spirit. That's what Paul means when he says, "The spirit of the prophets are subject to the control of the prophets." Each person can quench the Spirit, or we can be channels of the Spirit. Sometimes people can excuse their disruptive behavior by claiming, "The Holy Spirit came over me and made me do that." But that explanation isn't in alignment with Scripture. If you're disruptive, distracting, or harsh in your tone, that isn't God's fault, it's yours. This insight is important if we're going to come into agreement in prayer.

Agreement is an integral part of P3. It's much more than a general and passive consensus. It lays hold of the supernatural power of God. Let me explain. When Jesus was with His disciples at Caesarea Philippi, they had seen many miracles and heard Him teach about the kingdom for at least two years. Now He asked them, "Who do people say the Son of Man is?" The disciples said that the people thought He was John the Baptist (though I'm not sure how that works since they were both alive at the same time for quite a while), or Elijah, or Jeremiah, or another of the Old Testament prophets who had returned. Jesus then asked a more pointed question: "Who do you say I am?" Peter replied, "You are the Messiah, the Son of the living God."

Jesus affirmed Peter and explained the power of agreement:

> Jesus replied, "Blessed are you, Simon son of Jonah, for this was not revealed to you by flesh and blood, but by my Father in heaven. And I tell you that you are Peter, and on this rock I will build my church, and the gates of Hades will not overcome it. I will give you the keys of the kingdom of heaven; whatever you bind on earth will be bound in heaven, and whatever you loose on earth will be loosed in heaven." Then he ordered his disciples not to tell anyone that he was the Messiah. (Matthew 16:13–20)

This conversation took place where Baal had been worshiped centuries before, and more recently, where the Greeks had worshipped Pan. A cave is found there, and in the days of Jesus, the Greeks called it "the gates of Hell." Jesus had taken His disciples to the center and symbol of demonic authority to announce that the "gates of Hades will not overcome" His church. In Greek the word for church is "ecclesia." It was a term used for a community gathering, not just religious meetings. The ecclesia, the church, is the governing body to receive what God is saying and agree with one another to bind demonic powers and loose the power of God's Spirit.

When we pray in the Spirit with understanding, we then agree with one another to say, "Lord, let it be so! We agree with You and with one another to bind the enemy and turn on the mighty spigot of Your blessings for Your glory!" What does this look like? As we pray and share, we agree to bind fear and oppression, racism and bitterness, and we release God's love, peace, power, forgiveness, and joy. This is how we affirm and agree in our prayer.

As we pray and share, we agree to bind fear and oppression, racism and bitterness, and we release God's love, peace, power, forgiveness, and joy.

As I've used this form of prayer with our church board, I've been very encouraged by the response. Dr. Paul Brooks is a professor of theology who is also one of our board members and an elder in our church. One day after a board meeting, he reminded me of the gathering that took place when Peter and John were released from prison after they were arrested for healing a man in the name of Jesus. Luke puts us in the scene:

On their release, Peter and John went back to their own people and reported all that the chief priests and the elders had said to them. When they heard this, they raised their voices together in prayer to God. "Sovereign Lord," they said, "you made the heavens and the earth and the sea, and everything in them. You spoke by the Holy Spirit through the mouth of your servant, our father David:

'Why do the nations rage
	and the peoples plot in vain?
The kings of the earth rise up
	and the rulers band together
against the Lord
	and against his anointed one.'

Indeed Herod and Pontius Pilate met together with the Gentiles and the people of Israel in this city to conspire against your holy servant Jesus, whom you anointed. They did what your power and will had decided beforehand should happen. Now, Lord, consider their threats and enable your servants to speak your word with great boldness. Stretch out your hand to heal and perform signs and wonders through the name of your holy servant Jesus." (Acts 4:23–30)

Paul said he wondered, when Luke wrote, "... they raised their voices together in prayer to God" and "they said," if this might have been a P3 kind of prayer with several people adding parts of it. It may be that one person voiced the prayer and everyone else agreed, or perhaps, just perhaps, a number of people had a part in the prayer. It appears that powerful Spirit utterances occurred, and someone interpreted it for the whole so there could be agreement and victory. Notice how this passage reveals an utterance that includes declaration, acknowledgement of the Holy Spirit, reliance upon Scripture, objectivity about the situation at hand, trust in the sovereign will of God, and intercessory cries for God to help the church respond with bold faith. One thing is certain: "After they prayed, the place where they were meeting was shaken. And they were all filled with the Holy Spirit and spoke the word of God boldly" (Acts 4:31). That's what happens when God's people are unified to tap into God's heart, God's will, and God's power. We've gotten a taste of that as our team has learned to pray in the Spirit, with understanding, and in agreement, and as many others have trusted God to speak through their families and teams, they've had the same sense that God is among them.

I don't know what took me so long, but God is doing something only He can do throughout Oaks Church and in churches across the country as they pray this way. Isn't that what our hearts long for?

Think about it:

1. Describe the importance of praying in the Spirit with understanding.

2. Describe the power of praying in agreement.

3. In what ways are you empowered to fight spiritual battles when you pray in agreement with the Lord and with other believers?

CHAPTER 3

SPEAK, LORD!

I've been asked to speak on P3 at a number of denominational events, as well as conferences and other gatherings. The person who invites me invariably asks me to explain the biblical foundation, and especially, the practical steps the leaders in the audience can take. Let me spell out these steps for a pastor leading a staff team, or in smaller churches, a team of key volunteers. We'll go back over some of the ground we covered in the last chapter when we examined the three elements of P3 prayer, but here, we'll dive in more deeply.

Know Your Audience

I would imagine that virtually every staff member of a Pentecostal or Charismatic church prays in tongues. But in a group of key volunteers in these churches, there might be someone who doesn't yet function in this gift. And many people, even on leadership teams, haven't prayed in the Spirit aloud in a small group. If we make the wrong assumptions, we'll create awkwardness.

You know your people. If you're sure your team is practicing the gift, you can move forward fairly quickly. If you're not sure, take the time to explain the theology and practice so that everyone feels comfortable.

Prepare Them

Explain what's going to happen in the next few minutes: you're going to summarize the P3 concept that as a team, you can pray in the Spirit, with understanding, and in agreement with God and each other. You might say, "It's going to be a new experience, and we're all learning, but it will enable us to tap into the heart and mind of God in a fresh and powerful way. You'll have some questions along the way. If you want to ask something before we actually begin, please ask. But while we're in the process of praying, hearing, and sharing, wait until we're finished to ask questions that come to mind. Are you ready? This is going to be great!"

Ask

Even if they don't need to ask for the gift of tongues, they can ask for the understanding or interpretation, just as Paul encouraged us (1 Corinthians 14:16). Jesus invites us to come "boldly to the throne of grace." He told His followers,

> "So I say to you: Ask and it will be given to you; seek and you will find; knock and the door will be opened to you. For everyone who asks receives; the one who seeks finds; and to the one who knocks, the door will be opened.

> "Which of you fathers, if your son asks for a fish, will give him a snake instead? Or if he asks for an egg, will give him a scorpion? If you then, though you are evil, know how to give good gifts to your children, how much more will your Father in heaven give the Holy Spirit to those who ask him!" (Luke 11:9–13)

I tell pastors to use this passage and say something like this to their team:

> Do you pick up the excitement in Jesus' voice, the sense of eager anticipation that God wants to open doors and bless those He loves? This applies to all kinds of good gifts, but especially to the Holy Spirit and the gifts of the Spirit.
>
> If you haven't yet received the gift of tongues, this would be a great day for it. Ask Him.
>
> If you haven't received the ability to understand what God is saying in your prayer language, this would be a great day to receive it. Ask Him for the gift of interpretation.

The pastor can lead them in these prayers, trusting that a good and kind Father will give what they've asked for. And then thank Him.[2]

Pray in the Spirit

To set the expectation, I tell the group,

> Now we're going to pray in the Spirit. We're only going to pray for about a minute and a half. In Acts 2, it says, "They spoke in tongues as the Spirit enabled them." Who spoke in tongues? They did. The Holy Spirit is going to pray through you, but you don't need to wait for Him to move. You can take the initiative to pray, and you can take the initiative to stop. I'll let you know when the time is about up. Okay, let's pray.

---

2   For a personal story and a biblical perspective about the struggle to receive the baptism of the Spirit, see "Now More than Ever" by Dr. Chris Railey in the appendix.

You may not need to explain the part about each person having the responsibility to activate or stop manifestations. Many people don't realize that Paul wrote about a "partnership" with the Holy Spirit in which we work together intimately with the Spirit rather than in a slavish relationship. We bring desire and initiative, as 1 Corinthians 12-14 shows three times (12:31; 14:1, 39). In 2 Corinthians 13:10 Paul blessed the church: "May the fellowship (partnership, or communion, or intimacy) of the Holy Spirit be with you all." Unfortunately, some denominations teach that it's always and only God's initiative. They're sure they can't determine when to start praying in tongues, and once they've begun and feel the Spirit moving, nobody is going to tell them to stop! And the more expressive the better! When people tell me that they can't start or stop on their own, I give them this analogy:

> If our family is on a long trip in the car and one of the children says, "I have to go to the bathroom," I'll say, "Can you hold it for about five minutes until we get to an exit, or do you have to go right now?" If the child can't hold it, there's one of two problems: immaturity or a physical problem like an upset stomach. In the same way, if people can't "hold it" and control themselves when they pray in the Spirit, there's a problem of immaturity or perhaps a psychological problem of seeking attention.

Let me be clear: this may not be a problem for many teams, but if it is, this analogy gives you an idea of how to address it. Paul reminded the Corinthians that when the gifts are in operation, "Everything should be done in a fitting and orderly way" (1 Corinthians 14:40). He also explained that "the spirit of prophets are subject to the control of prophets" (1 Corinthians 14:32), which means the person being used in the gifts has the ability to start and stop the gift.

To avoid an awkward and abrupt stop, a few seconds before I plan for the group to finish praying in the Spirit, I say, "Okay, take just a few more seconds." This simple comment lets them know it's time to wind down, and in a short time, the room is quiet.

(By the way, if I'm leading a larger group in P3 prayer, I don't hold the microphone while I'm praying in the Spirit. I put it down and walk away so my voice isn't any louder than anyone else in the room. Remember this if you teach P3 to a big room full of people.)

Hearing, Watching

As soon as the prayer ends, I explain,

Now we're going to see what God is revealing to each of us. God may have spoken to you while you were praying, or He may give you the interpretation now. Trust Him to communicate with you and give you understanding. Some of you have seen a vision. Others have received a passage of Scripture, or a word or a phrase has come to mind. Some have words of intercession or praise. Each of you can share it when you are ready.

When I initially teach people the concepts of P3, I ask them to frame the message God puts on their hearts in the first person, as God is speaking through them, personally and directly, to the person or into the situation. They aren't relating God's heart from a third person perspective, as in "He said He loves you . . ."; instead, they're channels of God's own communication directly to the person: "God is saying, 'I love you . . .'"

Be Ready to Write

Whether anyone else writes down the messages they've gotten from God, the leader does. This is the record of God revealing His mind about a person or a situation, and we don't want to lose any of it! Have some paper and a pen, or maybe your notes page on your phone, ready when people begin to share.

This is the record of God revealing His mind about a person or a situation, and we don't want to lose any of it!

Share the Word

When I see that most people are looking up and appear to be ready, I'll say, "Okay, let's share with each other what God has put on our hearts. When you're ready, tell us what God said to you or what He showed you."

You're not in any hurry, so don't worry if there's a pause between people sharing. Usually, after a few experiences with P3, the group finds its rhythm. If someone goes too long, I gently interrupt and say something like "Thanks, we've got it."

If I'm still writing what someone said and another person begins, I'll say, "Wait just a second while I write this one." And when I'm finished, I look up and smile, "Now . . ." It only takes a P3 or two for everyone to get the idea of how much time they take for sharing and how much time the leader needs to write each one.

Like any prayer meeting, if the sharing slows down, I may say, "Anyone else?" But there's no pressure on anyone. If someone doesn't get an inspiration from God, or if they don't want to share it, that's fine. It's up to them.

I seldom prompt anyone to share, but if I sense that someone is hesitant, I may ask in a gentle voice, "Would you like to tell us what God is stirring within you?" Sometimes, the person has one of the most profound things to share, and we would have missed it if he didn't tell us about it. But if he says, "No, not really," I smile and respond, "No problem."

If a statement isn't clear, I silently ask God if He wants me to try to clarify it. I may ask the person, "Tell us what you think God is revealing through that word (or phrase or vision)." Or God may prompt me to connect a word with a passage of Scripture. I try to make only as many comments as are absolutely necessary. Less is better.

Read It Back

When the last person who wants to share is finished, I read back every statement, vision, and Scripture in the order they were shared. I believe the order of what was shared is also under God's sovereign hand. It's a gradual unfolding, or to use the stadium metaphor, it's like each section of fans turning over their cards in succession, and only at the end do we see the full picture.

We don't have to force a single interpretation on the various things people share. In my experience, when I read them back to the group, the different components seem stitched together into a powerful expression of the heart of God. This is true whether we're praying for an individual, for the church, or for a specific need.

At this point I don't give any commentary on what I've read. It's not needed, and actually, it's not appropriate. If we believe God himself has spoken to each of us, His message is clear and powerful.

Activate and Affirm

After I read the words from each person, I gather the team together, usually standing, and I lead us in prayer because we haven't finished until we've prayed in agreement. I tell them, "Now it's time to activate our faith and receive what God wants to give us." I look at the paper I've written, and I ask God to make each word real in the person or the situation. I read slowly, but often with some emotion because the message God has given is so powerful.

If I'm praying for a person in the room, I ask her to hold her hands in a position of receptiveness. If I'm praying for a situation in the church, the members of the team hold their hands to receive God's blessing, truth, and power. After each statement, which they've now heard three times, they say, "Amen! (1 Corinthians 14:16)" or "Yes, Lord!" or "To Your glory, Jesus!" or any other statement of claiming faith.

This step is the final one in the P3 process: We first prayed in the Spirit, then we asked God for understanding and shared what He gave us, and now we're agreeing that the God of greatness and grace will fulfill His word whenever and however He chooses.

As I pray through the statements we've shared, we all ask God to bind evil and release His power to transform individuals, families, or situations, depending on what God has said to us. We're not just mouthing words; we're clinging to God to trust Him to fight for us and with us as we seek to advance His kingdom.

Celebrate

After the prayer of agreement to activate our faith, we step back and celebrate what God has said and done. It's usually not a formal prayer at all. I just look at everybody and say, "Thank You, Jesus! You did it again!"

And Then . . .

After we P3, we move forward with the staff meeting or prayer meeting with the confidence that God is with us and is speaking into everything we are doing. We often say, "At Oaks Church we don't open the agenda with prayer, we set the agenda with prayer." We don't want to just acknowledge God when we meet, we want to hear Him speak and lead us. For instance, immediately after we pray or later in the day, I'll talk to one of our staff about something that came out of P3 at the beginning of a staff meeting, and often, I'll email our board to let them know what God has said to us. When we have P3 with the board, I'll tell our staff what God said through the people on our board. Using P3 has revolutionized my leadership, our expectations, and the effectiveness of our church. We're more in tune with God than ever before.

At Oaks Church we don't open the agenda with prayer, we set the agenda with prayer.

Is this step by step plan the only way pastors can lead P3 times of prayer? Of course not, but this is the way God has led me to implement the principles He has taught me about prayer. I encourage you to use the process I've outlined as a jumping off point. Try it and see how God works in and through your team. I'm sure you'll find ways to make it your own, but be sure all three aspects are part of your prayer: pray in the Spirit, with understanding, and in agreement. Use it often, and expect God to give each person on the team a card to hold up. It may change everything for everyone on your team.

Think about it:

1. What questions come to mind as you read the practices in this chapter?

2. Which step seems especially challenging?

3. Which step seems particularly exciting?

CHAPTER 4

IT'S NOT JUST ME

One of the most exciting things that has happened in my life is seeing how God is using many, many others to lead P3 prayer. District superintendents, bishops of other denominations, pastors of large churches and small ones, and from people who have been Christians for fifty years and to junior high students—it's amazing to see God use them in such powerful ways. Let me tell you about a few of them.

Out of the Room

At one point about a year into our experiences with P3, one of our staff members made a mistake. It was a dumb mistake more than a sin, but it was still a problem we needed to address on the board. In preparing for the next board meeting, I didn't inform the board members about the situation. When we walked into the room, I said, "Okay, let's pray in the Spirit and see what God says to us." We prayed and I asked them to share.

The first person looked a little confused, but he said, "Pastor, I don't know that this applies to you, but I sense the Lord say, 'I love you with an unconditional and everlasting love.'"

Another one spoke up: "The enemy comes to steal, kill, and destroy. You're in a season of testing, and the enemy is coming against you to bring fear and doubt. I don't want you to try to figure it out on your own because it's a spiritual battle that can only be won by the power of the Holy Spirit. Trust Me in the battle because I've already won."

Others shared, also in the first person, as God was speaking through them:

"I came that you might have life and life abundantly. During this time, let Me speak to you. Let Me bring you the peace only I can give."

"I will keep you in perfect peace as you keep your mind stayed on Me. Do not look to the right or the left. Keep your eyes fixed on Me."

"I oppose the proud, but I give grace to the humble. I've called you into leadership to care for my flock. Lead My people with love, humility, and compassion."

"Be faithful in the calling I've given you. I've called you, and I'm birthing bigger dreams than you can imagine. Don't be afraid of the bigger dreams I'm giving you. As I was with Abraham, I'm with you to guide you along the right path. Continue to associate with people I've given you, and I'll give the increase."

"I'm telling you that great people doing great things will make mistakes on their way to a great harvest. Son, I don't condemn you, so don't waste time condemning yourself. There's no condemnation for those who are in Christ Jesus. You're My child, and I love you unconditionally. When you see yourself, you see your faults, weaknesses, and mistakes you've made. I recognize that you're imperfect, but when I look at you, I see who I've created you to be, and I'm pleased with you."

When they finished and I had written all their statements, the person who make the last statement felt compelled to repeat what the first one said: "Pastor, I don't think these are for you, but we're just sharing what God has put on our hearts." I read them to the board in order, and they were still confused.

When we finished, I asked the staff member to come in and sit with us. Without explaining why he was asked to come, I read the statements again and prayed to activate them in his life. After the first one, he was weeping. When I'd finished reading, we all took a deep breath because we realized God had done something magnificent in this man's life . . . and in all of us. I asked him to tell the board about his mistake, but now, all the shame and fear were gone because God had already proclaimed His undying love, forgiveness, and purpose in this man's life. We all got up and hugged him. Each one said something like, "We believe in you," "We love you," and "God has great plans for you. Never doubt it." It was one of the most affirming and healing experiences I've ever witnessed. And I'm sure the staff member will never forget how God used the people on our board to impart compassion, forgiveness, and hope for a bright future.

I'm sure the staff member will never forget how God used the people on our board to impart compassion, forgiveness, and hope for a bright future.

District Council

Superintendent John Wootten invited me to speak at the Ohio District Council. This is his account of what happened there and the impact the event had on his district.

Pastor Scott,

The day before approximately 400 Ohio pastors and spouses arrived for the retreat, we gathered our district ministry directors, presbyters and assistant presbyters and their spouses to pray for our pastors and churches. I lead us in a presentation and a season of prayer titled "10 Threats to Christian Unity." As we concluded, we divided the room of leaders into 10 groups so each group could intercede for protection against one of the threats (tradition, complacency, bitterness, etc.).

Before you began your first talk to us that evening, you asked for me for permission to do something somewhat unusual as it relates to the moving of the Spirit. I invited one of our executive presbyters, Dave Gross, to listen with me as you explained how you wanted to lead us to be more receptive to the Spirit. I took confidence in what you explained, and when Dave strongly affirmed it, too, I felt the clear "green light" for you to proceed. (Three years later, I firmly believe the fact that you humbly and thoughtfully asked for permission in advance was key to the Spirit honoring the gathering that night the way that He did.)

After your message that night, you explained to everyone that we were going to do something a little different. You instructed all the ministers and spouses to begin speaking in their heavenly language.

After an extended season of this chorus of tongues, I remember thinking that you were going to bring the prayer time to a close, but you encouraged us to keep praying for another minute or so. When you brought that season to a close, you gave a new instruction: "As we were praying, some of you sensed what the Spirit was saying. Many of you didn't, but some of you did. If you feel led to say in English what you just heard the Spirit saying in a heavenly language, speak it out so we can all hear. It might be a sentence, or it might be just a few words. Please, if that's you, share the interpretation the Spirit is giving you."

Men and women all over the ballroom began to do exactly as you instructed. For some, it was a few words. Others shared several phrases. Still others spoke an entire sentence. It was like you were directing an orchestra. You had to encourage some to hold still for a second until someone from the other side of the room finished. It was all beautiful and all powerful. Dozens of ministers and spouses stepped forward in obedience and shouted the interpretation so you and everyone in the room could hear.

After the last person finished, you pulled another surprise. You said, "Most of you probably didn't notice, but as these brothers and sisters were sharing, I was writing each statement down. Many times, when a word from the Lord is shared, we enjoy it for a moment or even a season, but we fail to fully appreciate it and act on the Spirit's leading because we don't make a record of what was said. Tonight, I'm going to read back for you in one expression what dozens of you just shared individually."

This was the message you read to us:

> I am unifying you for what's about to come. I am sending angels to oversee you . . . I am opening streams in the desert . . . for a new breakthrough of growth . . . new life . . . I am sending a great light in the darkness...it will pierce the darkness....no weapon forged against you will prosper . . . I'm changing the way you think . . . I am doing a new thing . . . I am destroying the yoke . . . the yoke that is on you and your family . . . I am breaking the fear of man . . . it has to go . . . chains are coming off . . . Warriors ARISE!!!! I will cover you . . . for I am the God of victory, not defeat . . . I am calling everyone from the North, South, East and West . . . I will give you clarity on what to do and what to say . . . I AM STILL KING, I AM STILL KING, I AM STILL KING! The enemy has been defeated . . . my foot has crushed his head . . . again I tell you no weapon forged against you will prosper . . . I will cover the earth with my Glory . . . and you do not need to be afraid . . . I will be with you . . . I will anoint you . . . I will empower you . . . I will give you the words to say and you will not be empty or dry . . . My power is made perfect in your weakness . . . I am warring against unbelief . . . Believe in me . . . I go before you . . . I go behind you . . . there is no need to fear! The Battle is already Won! I AM THE GREAT I AM!

As you shared this word, there was a powerful response. Our leaders (the ones who had prayed earlier in the day for unity) felt "chills" when the first words were "I am unifying you for what's about to come!" After the retreat was over, you sent me an email with this prophetic word. Over and over again, in the months and years since, I have shared that message in our churches and repeated it numerous times at area and statewide gatherings of our ministers and leaders. Every time, there is a powerful response. Typically, several ask me if they can have a copy, which I'm happy to provide.

All I can say is that God is faithful to His word, whether it was in writing or whether it was spoken aloud. We asked God for unity, and in the P3 prayer time you led, God answered in ways that were immediately astonishing and ultimately sustaining.

A Wider Impact

After our staff and board had been using P3 prayer for a while, it was obvious that it was time to share it with a wider audience. I taught it in a seven-week series on Wednesday nights. When I announced it in church services, I explained that it was going to be a laboratory—in other words, we were going to practice what we were learning. About 300 people came. On the sixth night, I explained, "We don't just listen to God and speak prophetic words in church services. God wants to use us wherever we go. However, the words need to have Starbucks and Wal-Mart value. That means we speak God's truth in normal language and a normal tone of voice to normal people. When we're interacting with people at work, in the neighborhood, in school, and at the grocery store, we don't have to stop and stand aside to speak in tongues. We can pray silently for a short while—so short they don't even notice—and ask God to give us His message to share. We're walking in the Spirit all day every day."

I told them, "I want you to find a partner, and next Wednesday night, we're going out to interact with people in the community, and we're going to practice P3 to get God's leading. Before you go, you'll pray, and God will show you where to go, who to meet, and what to say. And God will use you to change lives. Don't worry. It'll be great. God has spoken to you in the last few weeks, and He'll speak to you next Wednesday night too." And I added, "If any of you don't want to go out, come to the church and pray for those who are going. That's a vital part of what we're doing. Don't miss it." About 70 of the 300 paired up to go out, and the rest committed to come and pray. Before we went out, we all met and prayed together that God would lead and use us.

I had no idea how this was going to go. I'd never done anything like this in my life, and I knew I had to be an example of courage and kindness for our people. The next Wednesday morning, I prayed, "Lord, it's happening tonight, and I don't know where to go or what to do. Will you show me?"

I prayed in the Spirit, and I asked God to speak to me. He gave me this to write down: "African-American single woman with two kids checking out at HEB (these are grocery stores all over Texas) at 7:53 pm." I still have the exact wording on the Notes page on my phone. Instantly, I thought, *Man, if this happens, it'll be really cool. If it doesn't, at least I'm trying to hear from God and obey Him.*

Instantly, I thought, "Man, if this happens, it'll be really cool. If it doesn't, at least I'm trying to hear from God and obey Him."

That night, my partner was a no-show! I was on my own. I was going to show up at HEB no matter what, but there was a problem. Before the service, I asked a missionary from Kenya come to the front to pray for those who were going out. He prayed . . . and prayed . . . and prayed. I kept looking at my watch as the time went by. I vividly imagined how fast I'd have to drive if he finished praying now, and then now, and then now. I'm not kidding, he prayed for about 30 minutes! At that point, I interrupted him and said, "Amen! Amen! Thank you, brother. It's time for us to go out."

I turned to my wife Jenni and her sister Angie and said, "Hey, come with me!"

They asked in unison, "Where are we going?"

"Don't worry about that." I hurried them along. "Hurry up! We don't have much time!"

We ran to the parking lot and jumped in the car. Jenni asked, "What in the world is going on?"

I told her, "We have to be at HEB by 7:53."

Jenni looked at her watch and said, "Uh, Scott, I don't think we're going to make it."

"Oh, we're going to get there."

"What are we going to do when we get to HEB?"

I smiled, "There's an African-American lady with two children who's checking out at 7:53."

Jenni and Angie looked at me like I had lost my mind. I was flying through traffic, but I told them about God speaking to me that morning as I prayed for direction, and that's the message He revealed to me. They probably still thought I'd lost it, but at least they understood my rush to the store.

I sped into a parking space at 7:52, and I ran inside. Jenni and Angie were right behind me. They didn't want to miss this! I looked at the first register. A white couple in their 60s. The second register. An older man. I quickly walked past the third, fourth, and fifth ones. At the sixth register stood a black lady with a basket full of groceries, and two kids were hanging on it. I walked slowly up to the lady and said, "Ma'am, have you paid yet?"

She looked more than a little surprised that a stranger would appear out of nowhere and ask such a strange question. "No, no, I haven't," she answered as she stared at me. Then she said, "Why do you ask?"

"The Lord sent me here to buy your groceries . . . and to give you a word. If you'd let me be obedient to the Lord, I'd like to do that."

Now she was looking at me like Jenni and Angie had looked at me in the car. I had nothing to lose, so I explained, "This morning as I prayed, I sensed the Lord tell me He wanted me to go to HEB at 7:53 tonight to meet an African-American lady with two children. I'm pretty sure that's you."

She reacted, "Oh no! You can't pay for all this. There are too many groceries in my cart."

I smiled, "Please. I'd love to." I put my credit card on the counter, and the attendant took it. She looked like I'd invaded earth from another planet, but she still took my card. I turned back to the lady, "When you've checked out, can I take a minute to tell you what God wants to say to you?"

"Sure."

A few minutes later, she had all her bags in the cart, and the attendant gave my card back to me. We walked over to the spot where Jenni and Angie were watching all this unfold. I introduced Jenni and Angie, and she introduced herself and her two kids. She looked at me. I'm sure she was thinking, *This is going to be good!* Her children were still and quiet. I said, "The Lord told me to tell you that He sees you and He loves you. He knows you have hopes and dreams for your children, just like He has hopes and dreams for you. He loves you, and the future is bright. He's going to bless you and lead you. Don't doubt it."

I paused for a second, and then I told her, "God also told me to tell you that he's going to heal you. Are you sick?"

"No," she answered. "I feel good."

I replied, "Huh. Okay. I guess I missed that one."

She then said, "Well, I guess you could pray for me. I'm going in for surgery next Tuesday."

"Yeah, maybe that's it! I think that counts!"

She laughed, "I think so too."

I said, "If you don't mind, I want to pray for you right now. If God put you on my heart this morning and told me to find you here at this exact time, I think He wants to do something wonderful in your life."

I put my hand on her shoulder, and I led the six of us in prayer for her healing. We parted with the powerful sense that God had led us to meet at that time and place for that reason.

When Jenni, Angie and I got back in the car, Jenni said what all of us were thinking, "Wow! That was amazing!"

It was an incredible time for people in our church to use P3 to guide us to touch the lives of people.

When we got back to the church, people shared how God had led them and given them just the right words for the people they met. It was an incredible time for people in our church to use P3 to guide us to touch the lives of people. It was something we'd never forget, but it was also something we knew we could do again and again.

Deliverance

When I spoke at a chapel service at Oral Roberts University, the president, Dr. Billy Wilson, asked me to speak on a chapter from my book, *Clear the Stage.* When I finished, about a half dozen students came up to talk to me. After I talked with the third one, the number had grown to about 15. A few minutes later, there were probably 40. Then, there were about 150. When I got to about the fifteenth person, the girl next to her fell on the floor in convulsions. This wasn't epilepsy; it was a demon. A group of students and I stood around her and prayed in the Spirit. Then I leaned down and whispered to the demonic force, "I tell you right now: Shut up! You won't steal any attention from what God is doing here. In the name of Jesus, be still." Then I addressed the girl, "Don't worry, sweet girl. We'll take care of this."

Instantly, she stopped shaking and was calm. I turned to the dean, who had rushed over to help, and asked him to take care of the girl. He and several students helped her up and took her to a secluded place where they could pray.

I continued to talk to students in the line. After about 30 minutes, it was time for them to go to class. There were about 10 students still in line, so I said, "Guys, instead of talking to each of you individually, let me show you how to pray in the Spirit, with understanding, and in agreement. I call it P3. Would that be okay with you? Are you in?" They all agreed.

By this time, the dean had walked up and joined us. I gave them a one-minute explanation of the principles and practice of

P3, and we started praying in the Spirit. After a minute, I said, "Okay, what's God saying to you?"

The girl on my left immediately said, "I feel like God is saying, 'No matter what's going on in your life, I'll bring you peace. I'll break the power of Hell and set the people free.'"

The other students and the dean voiced what God had put on their hearts. I wrote them all down and read them back. Everybody was crying. It was a powerful time for all of us. One of them said, "How'd you know to do that?"

I explained that we'd been using P3 in our church for a while, and it had been incredible. We all hugged, and the students left for class. At that moment, the dean walked up and smiled, "Is that crazy or what?"

I had no idea what he was talking about. He saw that I wasn't tracking, so he asked, "Do you not recognize the girl who was on your left?"

I shook my head, "No, should I?"

"It's the girl who was convulsing on the floor a little while ago!"

In our P3 prayer, the Lord spoke to her that He's bringing peace and victory over the forces of darkness, and this message wasn't just for her, but for all of us in the group.

She had changed so much in those few minutes since the dean and the students picked her up off the floor. In our P3 prayer, the

Lord spoke to her that He's bringing peace and victory over the forces of darkness, and this message wasn't just for her, but for all of us in the group.

Amazing. Simply amazing.

Clearing Away the Confusion

One of our staff members recently sent me this note:

Pastor Scott,

Since I was 10 years old, I have been filled with the Holy Spirit. However, until P3 was introduced to me, the baptism in the Holy Spirit had been a confusing, supernatural thing that was very hard to explain and even harder to fully comprehend.

P3 has taken something that confused me and has been hard to understand and turned it into a part of my everyday life that produces fruit and gives me direction for living each day. Living a life in the Spirit is now a natural-supernatural part of my life.

Amazing Peace

As I taught P3 to our church, a lady named Barb came to me with some questions. Actually, they were more than questions. The idea of hearing from God in this way terrified her. She had grown up in another denomination that doesn't practice all the gifts, and she was wary of preachers on television who claimed to hear direct messages from God, heal everyone, and shouted when they preached. As she explained her concern, she said, "When I came to The Oaks, you taught me about the gift of tongues. I received the gift, and it has meant a lot to me." She continued, "I assumed we can't interpret when we speak in tongues. When you told us that we could ask God for the interpretation as we pray in the Spirit, I thought, 'Oh no! Not my sweet pastor!' I'm here because I trust you and I love you. I'm scared, but I'm open to you teaching me about all this."

We took plenty of time to go through the passages of Scripture. She asked questions, and I answered them. When we finished, she said, "Okay, I see what the Word is saying, and I understand now how you got to the principles of P3 . . . but it still makes me feel uncomfortable."

I smiled, "Let's go try it."

She looked panicked, "What do you mean?"

Our conversation happened on a Wednesday night, and the church was full of about 400 teenagers. I told Barb, "Let's go down to where the teenagers are meeting. I'll ask some of them to use P3 and pray for you. Would that be okay?" She nodded.

We walked downstairs and into the hall where kids were coming in. I said, "Hey!"

A bunch of them responded, "Hey, Pastor!"

I asked, "How many of you know how to P3?"

Several of them raised their hands. I picked six of them at random and said, "Will you come with me to practice P3?"

They were eager to join Barb and me, but of course, they had no idea that Barb was apprehensive about this kind of prayer. They followed us to an empty room. I introduced Barb, and I asked, "I'd like for us to pray for Barb. Who wants to facilitate P3?"

One of the students instantly volunteered, "I will." She asked Barb if she wanted to get her phone ready to record the sharing. "You might want to have it so you can listen to what God says to you tonight." Then she asked the group to pray in the Spirit.

A minute or so later, the student leader let them stop, and she invited people to share the message God had given them. They were all words of encouragement, affirmation, and love. This is what the student wrote down:

> Strength—Psalms 46: We shall not fear, God is our strength. I am your refuge. I am holding everything, you don't need to worry. You are qualified for what you are stepping into. I am going to take you places. I will give you strength to rise above. Wait on me and I will renew your strength. Don't try to do things the old way as the new comes, I will equip you with new ways.

> Be at peace. When you rest in me and in my goodness, your heartbeat will be in sync with Mine. Your steps will be led. You're mine, so be confident and rest knowing I am leading you and strengthening you.

From the first person's message from God, Barb started crying. When everyone was finished sharing, the leader read the statements back to Barb. She cried even more. Then the leader told Barb, "Miss Barb, people often posture themselves to receive the blessings we pray into them. If you'd like to do that, you can." Barb held her palms up as the leader prayed each message to activate Barb's faith in what God had spoken. By now, Barb was balling, but they were tears of joy and relief, not pain or fear. The students hugged her.

The students walked out and went to their meeting. I turned to Barb and asked simply, "What do you think?"

Wiping tears off her cheeks, she smiled, "That was powerful."

I told her, "It's really good to understand the truth from the Bible, but you just experienced God loving you through these students. That's God's truth about His grace and strength . . . with skin on."

Several months later, she wrote me:

> I read this [the statements God gave the students that day] every month or so. It continues to touch and strengthen me because it's from "my Daddy"; tailor-made for me in this season. What's interesting is that I was receiving some of this in my prayer life as well ("I got this, just trust me."), however, experiencing a P3 group validated it and gave more ("You're qualified." "I will equip you with new ways."), and it was much more powerful and edifying. I continue to grow in confidence and trust in hearing from God individually. (I'm not a baby sheep, but maybe a junior higher sheep.) The P3 group made any inadequacy I may feel a non-factor, therefore increasing my faith and trust (1 John 5:14-15). Thanks for all you do, Pastor.

This Works!

I received this letter from Dr. Doug Witherup, a professor at Southeastern University. My son Dillon was in his class when they studied spiritual gifts.

> You can't go back. You can't experience the fullness of the life-changing, life-giving power of God through the gifts and presence of the Holy Spirit and then go back to a form of Christianity that's less.
>
> I tried. It doesn't work.
>
> It all goes back to a sweltering hot Sunday morning in August of 1992. It was the summer after my junior year of high school. How I ended up on a mission trip to the Dominican Republic—other than the providence of God and the persistence

of my youth pastor—I'll never know. It sure wasn't because I was a model Christian. I was probably barely a Christian, if that's even possible.

It's not that I didn't love God. I did. And I loved my parents. And my church. But I also loved feeling popular. And parties. I thought I could live a double life, and no one would be the wiser. I was able to fool a lot of people, but of course, I couldn't fool God, and I sure couldn't fool myself. I was miserable. I had lost all joy and vigor and drive for life.

So, I found myself in a Sunday morning service in Santo Domingo, pouring out sweat. (In the 80s, silk shirts were a fashion disaster, especially in temperatures and humidity of 90 degrees and 90 percent. Wearing one that morning was quite a mistake.) Pastor Jim Grove was preaching on the baptism of the Holy Spirit and gave an altar call for people to receive the gift. When someone asked me if I wanted to be prayed for, I agreed. When Pastor Jim laid his hands on me, all I remember was falling to my knees under the power of God and a spiritual language pouring out of me. When I got up, I wasn't the same.

You can't go back.

But I tried.

The first two years of my undergrad college years were filled with skeptics, cynics, and theological jargon aimed more at questioning the validity of the exercise of the power of God than releasing faith to receive it. I'm not blaming anyone. It was my fault. I should have been more discerning about who I hung around. I should have guarded my heart, but I allowed the cynicism to creep in. And I witnessed first-hand things done in the name of ministry that I was skeptical of at best . . . and at worst were probably manipulations of the power of God. Eventually,

I left a Spirit-filled university not sure that I really believed in or wanted the gifts of the Spirit.

That all changed the day I took a short cut.

When I began in youth ministry, my office was on one side of the auditorium and the finance office was on the other. Instead of walking through the lobby and the hallways, sometimes I took a shortcut across the auditorium. On one of those shortcuts, I just happened to run into Phil Bennett, who was on staff as our prayer pastor. Phil is a gentle and kind man, and an absolute prayer warrior and man of God. He stopped me and asked me if he could share something with me. For the next fifteen minutes, Phil shared with me some things that the Lord was showing him—about me! I was shocked. Stunned. I'd never seen anything like this. Had he been spying on me? Reading my journal? How could he possibly know what was going on in the inner depths of my soul? (Although I was raised Pentecostal, I had never experienced words of knowledge.) This "chance" conversation sent me on a journey to seek the Lord like never before and recover everything that I felt like I had lost, neglected, or turned my back on related to spiritual gifts and the power of God.

For the next twenty years of ministry, I found myself living in the tension of 1 Corinthians 12-14. In chapter 12, the Apostle Paul is passionate about spiritual gifts. In chapter 13, he is passionate about reaching the lost. And then Paul develops a conclusion that seems to be quite lost in most ministry circles today: a corporate worship service that has both the power of God exercised through spiritual gifts and the power of His grace that reaches the lost—and they are not mutually exclusive.

Over the decades, I have watched some of my friends in pastoral leadership abandon their Pentecostal roots. I saw some go the seeker-sensitive route. I saw others identify with the neo-Reformed movement. Most found a place somewhere in the middle: being Charismatic in their worship expression and theology but not fully in practice. I was one of these people. We raise our hands in worship, believe in the baptism of the Holy Spirit and the fullness of the gifts, but we had seen too much weird stuff and we didn't want that in our services.

After serving the same church for twenty years, from summer intern to youth pastor to associate pastor, I found myself leading the church that I loved and had felt called to all my life. And I wanted it all. I wanted the fullness of God in the power of His Spirit. And I wanted to reach the lost. I wanted someone who was far from God to be able to experience the service and not be freaked out.

I wanted everything that God had for us. But I also wanted it to be done decently and in order. And I wanted unbelievers to be able to be in our services and understand what was going on. We seldom had utterances in tongues with interpretations during a Sunday morning worship service, but at times they did occur. Our facilities made it especially challenging. Our broadcast location is an 1100 seat auditorium with a main floor and balcony, so it was difficult for people to see or hear each other from different parts of the room.

One Sunday morning someone attempted to speak out in tongues. I felt in my spirit that the timing was off, so I went on stage and lovingly brought direction and teaching to that moment. People were so kind and gracious so there were no complications or disunity that occurred from that moment. But internally, I was torn up. This event surfaced the glaring deficiency in our services. I had no idea how we could practice the gifts in our corporate worship in this facility.

To find answers, I dove into 1 Corinthians again. And I prayed. It just so happened that I was traveling to Lakeland, Florida, to teach a week of a master's degree cohort. I was teaching a homiletics course. We began the week with the question, "If Jesus was the greatest preacher who ever lived, what can we learn from Him?" I explained Jesus' preaching methodology, showing that out of Christ's 146 preaching episodes in the four gospels, He usually used stories, questions, and encounters. Eighty percent of the time that Jesus spoke about the gospel, He was not just giving "seven concepts to consider this morning," but rather, He combined His teaching some type of encounter: a miracle, a spiritual gift in operation, or a specific call to action. As a class, we dove into the question: "What does this look like in a large corporate worship gathering?"

There were two students in my class from The Oaks Church, Dillon and Christina. I was familiar with the church and their pastor. I knew that Pastor Scott Wilson was one of the few mega-church pastors of a large, thriving, growing, city-reaching church who operated in spiritual gifts in their corporate gatherings. I asked Dillon and Christina, "Would you tell me more of what do you guys do in your worship services?"

More than I could have imagined, they were prepared to give an answer! They talked us through the P3 process. At the end, Dillon raised his hand, "Professor, this is your class. Whatever direction you want to go is fine, but could we practice what we've been talking about? Could we try this out? I'll lead it and show you what I'm talking about."

"Yes," I told him. "We absolutely can."

For the next three hours, the class turned into a prayer meeting. We prayed, prophesied, operated in the gifts of the spirit, and cried together. Dillon not only led, but he taught. He showed us how to do it while he was leading us. And then others led it while Dillon guided them. It was a naturally supernatural ministry lab. In fact, this was one of the most beautiful experiences I have had in ministry. Words of knowledge were given over people that were unbelievably spot on. For instance, here are some of the examples of what occurred in class that day. These are not the full P3's, but just some highlights:

- One of the students saw a picture of an individual as a Spartan warrior leading a vast army. The student being prayed for became emotional as he shared that during one undergrad class, his teacher asked students to vocalize some of their God-dreams, and the student shared that his prayer was that God would use him to lead an army of worshippers.

- As we prayed for a young lady in the class, one person saw a picture of a dry-erase board that was completely clean. Through her tears, the young lady explained that even though she was in ministry, there were some things in her life from years ago for which the enemy had continually condemned her. She experienced a wave of God's forgiveness.

- For another young lady, someone saw a picture of blueberries. She shared that every morning her drink of choice is blueberry tea. She said that God was reminding her how much He loves her and that He sees the smallest details of her life.

- For a young man, someone saw him in a barber's chair "getting a fresh cut." He shared how the Lord had recently used him to lead his barber to Christ.

- For me, part of the P3 was the message: "I am taking you from a light bulb . . . to a new 'Alexa' light. Just like 'Alexa' is voice activated and changes color (which is more than a normal light bulb can do) . . . I want to give you an upgrade. This upgrade will bring new experiences and life . . . not just for you, but for the people who are in the room with you . . . where your light is shining." I had just received an Alexa as a gift. The P3 continued, "These new resources will be like a peaceful spring rain . . . bringing life to you." One of my "life leadership verses" is Proverbs 16:15, "Good-tempered leaders invigorate lives. They are like spring rain and sunshine." The messages from God ended with this assurance: "All of this will feel natural. You don't have to be afraid . . . it will be like riding a bike or playing baseball for you." Those two images couldn't have resonated more. They were two of my favorite things to do a kid.

It didn't stop in the class. I immediately took the P3 process back to my church. I taught our staff and our church. and we began to practice it together. Here are some of our P3's and the results:

We were in a meeting to prepare to do a re-launch of our small groups. For decades, groups had struggled in our church. We had tried multiple variations, but nothing really seemed to catch on. We were getting ready to do a re-launch, and as a part of that, we did a P3. (For each of these P3's, I'll share the images/ words we received as well as the final word.)

Images:

- a winding road with an exit on it
- work boots
- a "plus" sign that turned into a "multiply" sign
- the words "healing" and "connection"
- a tree
- a rainbow with a pot of gold at the end

The final word:

"I am bringing you to an exit in the road. It is new territory, so you will have to put on work boots to cut a new path. (These boots will also bring protection.) These groups will move you from addition to multiplication. They will bring healing and connection and will bring the full spectrum of my high definition promises that will change family trees."

Since the P3 about groups, a sermon series, and the restructuring of our leadership, our groups have gone from 30 groups with about 300 involved to over 130 groups with over 1000 involved in about a year. They are thriving and bringing the change to our church and community—exactly like the P3 described.

Another P3 involved our Mothers' Day sermon. For this week, I was tag-team preaching with our women's pastor and a young lady who is one of our Southeastern University students.

Images:

- a picture of a clean slate
- a rose that was both red and white
- a shovel digging deep and hitting water
- the words, "Call out to dry bones, 'come alive!'"

The final word:

"In your DESERT, I am the shovel that has been digging in the desert. What you thought was a dry and barren season is actually a digging season. I am teaching you to find water at a deeper level."

"In your WILDERNESS, I am placing you as a cut rose in the water. But even a rose in the water loses its petals. At first you were panicked and upset. You thought something was dying. You thought you were losing something. It's not and you weren't. It was a season. Let the petals fall. It is not a season of loss but a season of beauty. I am using this as a flower girl prepares the way for the bride to prepare the world for Jesus."

"In your WASTELAND, I am giving you a clean slate. I am calling to the seemingly dead places in your life and calling to the dry bones, 'Come Alive!'"

It was a powerful message. We read the P3 at the end of the service and presented each lady in the audience with a white and red-tipped rose as a symbol of the blood of Christ and their purity as a result of what Christ did on the cross.

In June, we celebrated our 60th anniversary as a church. We are blessed to have had only four lead pastors over the six decades. Our founding pastor, who is my spiritual grandfather, still attends on Sunday mornings and is the biggest cheerleader of the church and our future. My predecessor now serves as our District Superintendent and is one of the key mentors in my life. We wanted this not to be just a time of celebration, but a spiritually significant moment. In our P3 during our preparation for the celebration, we saw images and God spoke a final word:

Images:

- a path
- a portal
- a catapult
- a stone
- a ring of fire
- Iron Man's armor coming together
- a water tower

The final word:

"The 60th is not the path, it's a portal; it is a point of transition, a stepping stone, that will catapult you through a ring of fire to the next level and next dimension. I will unify the generations and the city (like Iron Man's armor coming together). I have a water tower supply for the city that I want to release."

This P3 formed many aspects of our weekend celebration. Friday night was a worship concert featuring Travis Greene. (Quick backstory: we were struggling a bit to find our voice and identity of our worship team. Our church is highly multi-cultural, so what was our sound? Elevation? Hillsong? Gospel? And we also were at times struggling to walk the line between excellence in production and flowing in the Spirit.) During this concert, the Lord used Travis to show our team a prophetic picture of the future of worship ministry for our church—a combination of rock and gospel, a combination of excellence in production and the power of God. This insight is guiding our path forward. Our two new worship pastors are a black young lady and a white guy. The picture they present to our church every week is a picture of who we are.

On Sunday we gave an illustrated message during which we told the story of one of our ministries: Corner Field Market feeds over 1000 needy families each month. We traced the story through three generations, from the three ladies who started the ministry out of their closets and $100 in cash to the 10,000 square foot facility today. We ended with one of our Southeastern University students who is training to be in ministry and who volunteers at CFM. She shared how her introduction to our church was through receiving food from CFM during a time of need in her family. Both the worship concert and sermon brought the generations together and catapulted our church through the ring of fire toward the future.

I could go on. We have done P3's during our Wednesday night Deeper services and prayed for people as words of knowledge came for specific areas of healing. We have done them during staff meetings and board meetings. Our departmental ministries do them as they prepare for upcoming retreats. We have done them on our annual staff "Pray and Play" retreat as the Lord shapes His direction for us for the upcoming year.

I see the P3 process as part of what the Apostle Paul was describing in 1 Corinthians 12. It is a wonderful tool to do spiritual gifts in a way that is naturally supernatural. I encourage those who want to experience all of the power of God but don't know how it works practically—this is an answer. If you're afraid of going back to "less than," I have good news for you. You don't have to!

These are just a few samples of how God has used P3. By the time you read this, there will be plenty more stories to share.[3]

---

3   For more insights about using P3 with a broader audience in your church, see "A View from the Pew" by Dr. Paul Brooks in the appendix.

Think about it:

1. Which of the stories is most meaningful to you? Explain your answer.

2. Can you see yourself and your team becoming part of the story of P3? Why or why not?

CHAPTER 5

PASTOR THE PROCESS

In the years we've been using P3 as our model of prayer, and as I've taught it to our denominational executives, leaders of other denominations, pastors, missionaries, team leaders, and group leaders, I've been asked plenty of questions. A few of them are theological, but most are practical. My answers are specific to the questions, but underneath them all is the encouragement for those of us facilitating this kind of prayer to *pastor the process.* Here are answers to some of the most common questions and concerns:

"I can't do what you do."

As I've taught and led times of P3 prayer, some leaders have remarked, "Pastor Scott, you're obviously gifted in doing this, but I'm not. I can't do it." I assure them that's not the case. My staff have learned and now regularly practice it, every team in our church uses it, high school students, parents, and pastors all over the country are using it. You don't need a special gift to lead a group in P3 prayer. You just have to understand the basic principles and be obedient to the Lord. If you have a track record of praying and listening to God, you're ready to lead this kind of prayer.

"What does it mean to 'judge' in prayer?"

Paul instructed, "The spirits of prophets are subject to the control of prophets" (1 Corinthians 14:31). As we lead P3 prayer, God gives us discernment. All of us are "double exposures" of the old Adam and the new man in Christ, so every time we communicate what God puts on our hearts, there's some blend of flesh and Spirit. For immature believers, there might be a greater mixture of flesh than in those who have walked with God and been refined by fire over a longer time, but even then, there's always an element of flesh in our understanding and communication. When I'm leading P3 prayer and hearing people share the message God has given them, it's part of my God-given role to discern, to "judge" which part of their statements are of God and which parts are of the flesh. This isn't the time for rebuke and correction! Almost always, I ignore the fleshly part and accentuate the Spirit part.

Again, this isn't some kind of spiritual gift that's reserved for only a few. When we hear people share what God has taught them or how He's leading them, we often think, *Man, that's really odd,* or *Wow, that rings true!* That's what I do when I listen to people who are communicating their understanding of what God said to them as they prayed in the Spirit.

Sometimes, I have to work hard to figure out what God is saying through someone. At a meeting of pastors I was leading, when it was time to share, the first one stated boldly, "I saw an angel. It was a dove."

I don't usually make any comments as people share. It's too sacred to interrupt unless I sense it's necessary, but this time, it felt necessary. I asked, "Brother, what was God saying through that vision?"

He didn't miss a beat: "I saw an angel. It was a dove."

I thanked him, and waited for the next person to speak. He said, "God is saying, 'I'm here with you, and where I am, you'll find peace.'"

I think that's the message the first pastor was trying to communicate, but the second person made it clear. Every gift, talent, or skill is developed by its use, and the ability to discern what God is saying through people becomes sharper as you practice it. If at all possible, make no comment at all. Let the statements stand as God's voice to the person or into the situation, but rarely, and only when necessary, step in to ask for clarification, or clarify a statement yourself.

Let the statements stand as God's voice to the person or into the situation, but rarely, and only when necessary, step in to ask for clarification, or clarify a statement yourself.

I've been in a prayer meeting when a pastor screamed out harsh condemnation for everyone in the room . . . except himself. He disrupted the meeting in a big way, but as I pastored the moment, I didn't match him decibel for decibel and snarl for snarl. I sensed that everyone there understood that this man was out of bounds and wasn't representing God in any way, so I just moved on to the next person. On another occasion in a large meeting when we practiced P3, a man shouted, "God is saying, 'I love you!'" but his tone was harsh. I whispered in to the microphone, "Yes, Lord, You love us." The people there understood that I was ratcheting down the man's intensity. After the meeting, I asked him to talk with me. I affirmed him that the message of God's love is wonderful and powerful, but I asked him, "Do you express your love to your wife that way?"

He looked shocked and blurted out, "No, of course not! I wouldn't talk to her like that."

"Why do you think God talked that way to us through you? Do you think He's angry at us?"

"No, not at all."

"Then tell me what happened."

He thought for a second and then told me, "Every time I've heard someone prophesy in church, they yelled really loud, so I thought that's the way you're supposed to do it. This is the first time I've ever tried to prophesy. To be honest, it felt kind of awkward."

I said, "Brother, I've got good news for you. You don't have to yell like that. In fact, I'd be glad if you didn't. Your tone of voice didn't match the words God was speaking to us."

The man looked intently at me. With a sigh of relief, he told me, "I'm so glad you talked to me . . . because that felt really stupid."

Should we have to teach people about something as foundational as prayer? Some people believe that it's fine for pastors to teach people about all kinds of biblical concepts, but their people should just magically get everything they need about prayer. That just doesn't make sense to me. If anything, we need to teach more carefully and boldly about how to connect to God, hear from Him, and respond to His voice. P3 has given us a framework to teach people how to pray in unity and with expectancy. We need to teach it, model it, and provide a lab for them to try it for themselves.

"What about people who use this prayer to call attention to themselves?"

It happens. We've all been in meetings of every kind when someone who is insecure tries to be the center of attention. They talk louder than others, make more dramatic statements than anyone else, and have to have the last word. In my experience, P3 defuses competition and pride. But even more, the process of focusing on God, of hearing from everyone who wants to share, and valuing each person equally, has a wonderful effect of modeling humility and unity. No one has the whole message, so no one dominates the time. The underlying premise of all Paul writes in 1 Corinthians 12–14 is that we're a body, and we only function well if look to Jesus as our head and work in beautiful unison with each other. This decentralizes responsibility to hear from God—which may be a threat to leaders who feel very uncomfortable if they're not in complete control. But let me assure you, it also takes a lot of pressure off because we don't feel pressured to have every answer.

Of course, it's certainly possible that someone doesn't get the memo about humility. In that case, you may want to talk to the person outside the meeting and go deeper than the behavior to uncover the source of insecurity that drives the behavior. As a group of people pray in the Spirit, with understanding, and in agreement, self-centeredness is usually eroded by the wonder that God has been among them.

Tempted to Skip

I hate to admit it, but there are times when I'm so over-whelmed with all the things on the agenda for our staff meeting that I think about saying a quick prayer and starting with the first item on the list. How dumb is that? Thankfully, I don't give in to this temptation very often. P3 prayer has become part of our culture and schedule, and it's so powerful than none of us want to miss it. But sometimes, the tyranny of the urgent whispers that we don't have time to hear from God. Just being honest . . .

Ways God Speaks

As we P3 in our staff meetings, it didn't take long for patterns to emerge: God seems to always give some people a vision or a picture, some usually share a passage of Scripture, and others typically have a phrase and sometimes just a word. There's nothing in the world wrong with that. God made some to be seers, some to hear primarily from the Word, and some to get a cryptic message. I would guess that personality plays a role. For instance, the ones who are more sensitive and artistic may receive visions. And experience may shape how we get messages from God. Perhaps those who are more steeped in the Scriptures are more in tune with passages that God wants to share through them.

God seems to always give some people a vision or a picture, some usually share a passage of Scripture, and others typically have a phrase and sometimes just a word.

Don't feel any pressure to ask people to vary how God speaks to and through them. The form of the message is up to God, not us.

Mystery or Clarity?

When I explain the theology undergirding P3, some people point to 1 Corinthians 14:2: "For anyone who speaks in a tongue does not speak to people but to God. Indeed, no one understands them; they utter mysteries by the Spirit." They ask, "If when I speak in tongues I'm talking to God, why are you asking me to trust God to speak to me?"

Yes, we certainly utter mysteries, but only a few verses later, Paul explains that they don't have to remain mysteries: "For this reason the one who speaks in a tongue should pray that they may interpret what they say. For if I pray in a tongue, my spirit prays, but my mind is unfruitful. So what shall I do? I will pray with my spirit, but I will also pray with my understanding; I will sing with my spirit, but I will also sing with my understanding" (1 Corinthians 14:13–15). This verse, this revelation, was the genesis for all I've learned and experienced in P3.

I don't believe God has given me "new truth." Not in the least. He has opened my eyes to see what has been there all along. I'm not sure why I didn't see it before, but I see it now: when we pray in the Spirit, God wants to give us understanding, and mysteries become discernible. But this shouldn't be new or odd in any way. When someone speaks in tongues in church and another person interprets, that's God giving understanding to the house. P3 is taking that principle into the smaller groups of teams, families, and small groups.

Why Pray Together?

Some have asked why we advocate praying in the Spirit together instead of letting each person have a private and personal
prayer closet. Certainly, individual prayer is important, and it's
the way we connect with God most often. But these chapters in 1
Corinthians, as well as all the "one another" passages in the New
Testament, loudly proclaim that we're part of a body with Christ
as the head. Praying together is how blood flows from one part
to the other, how ligaments and tendons hold the parts together,
how we hear from the head and respond in coordinated and powerful ways. As we pray in the Spirit together, and especially with
understanding and in agreement, we experience a deepening dependence on God and a rich interdependence on each other.

In another letter, the one to the Christians in Philippi, Paul
captures the essence of the vertical relationship with God and
the horizontal relationship with each other: "Therefore if you
have any encouragement from being united with Christ, if any
comfort from his love, if any common sharing in the Spirit, if any
tenderness and compassion, then make my joy complete by being
like-minded, having the same love, being one in spirit and of one
mind" (Philippians 2:1–2). We can experience this kind of unity
in other ways, but I've seen it displayed most powerfully in times
of P3 prayer as God gives each person a part of His message, and
the parts form a single, powerful message of encouragement and
direction.

The Pharisees were always trying to trap Jesus. At one point,
one of them, an expert in the law, asked Him, "Teacher, which is
the greatest commandment in the Law?"

Jesus answered, "'Love the Lord your God with all your heart
and with all your soul and with all your mind.' This is the first

and greatest commandment. And the second is like it: 'Love your neighbor as yourself.' All the Law and the Prophets hang on these two commandments" (Matthew 22:35–40). We can experience God's love in countless ways, but why not add P3? We can learn to love one another in all kinds of situations, but why not include the unifying power of P3? Is P3 the answer to everything? No, but it puts us in touch—in the Spirit and in union with each other—with the One who is the answer to everything.

The writer to the Hebrews warns and encourages us: "Let us hold unswervingly to the hope we profess, for he who promised is faithful. And let us consider how we may spur one another on toward love and good deeds, not giving up meeting together, as some are in the habit of doing, but encouraging one another—and all the more as you see the Day approaching" (Hebrews 10:23–25). As we trust God to speak to us and through us, I've seen people "spur one another on toward love and good deeds" more than ever before.

In all of this, I don't have to carry the burden of being the only one who hears from God. I'm the lead follower, and it's my role to create a time and place where all of us seek God with all our hearts, trust Him to speak to each of us, and share the parts so that the whole message inspires us, directs us, and strengthens us.

In Genesis 11, people built a ziggurat as a symbol of their pride and rebellion against God, but God confused them by giving them different languages. This resulted in division and separation, and it diminished the power of the people by breaking their unity. The counterpoint to that event is Pentecost when God gave a single message through different voices—a message of grace, dependence, and hope. At Babel, people were divided by language, and at Pentecost, the believers were united by tongues of fire that rested on each of them, allowing them to enter into the heart of God and empowering them to be all God wanted them to be.

My role is to lead, to encourage, and to equip my team and everyone who is interested to be integrally connected to Christ as our head so we function as a healthy body. Paul described the role of leaders and the impact of pointing people to Christ:

> So Christ himself gave the apostles, the prophets, the evangelists, the pastors and teachers, to equip his people for works of service, so that the body of Christ may be built up until we all reach unity in the faith and in the knowledge of the Son of God and become mature, attaining to the whole measure of the fullness of Christ.
>
> Then we will no longer be infants, tossed back and forth by the waves, and blown here and there by every wind of teaching and by the cunning and craftiness of people in their deceitful scheming. Instead, speaking the truth in love, we will grow to become in every respect the mature body of him who is the head, that is, Christ. From him the whole body, joined and held together by every supporting ligament, grows and builds itself up in love, as each part does its work. (Ephesians 4:11–16)

Praying in the Spirit, with understanding, and in agreement is a powerful way to build unity, to help people grow into maturity, to be strong against temptation and deception, and to work together for Christ's glory. In one of the songs of ascents, David wrote about the beauty and power of unity:

How good and pleasant it is
    when God's people live together in unity!
 It is like precious oil poured on the head,
    running down on the beard,
running down on Aaron's beard,
    down on the collar of his robe.
It is as if the dew of Hermon
    were falling on Mount Zion.
For there the Lord bestows his blessing,
    even life forevermore. (Psalm 133)

In this passage we see three benefits of coming into a prayer of unity: First, the anointing of the Spirit is symbolized by the oil poured on Aaron's head, which is the leadership of the congregation, and it flows down his face to his collar, which means the anointing affects everyone. Second, the dew of Hermon falling on Mount Zion symbolizes God's rich blessings. Hermon was a mountain in the lush part of northern Palestine, but Mount Zion was in the arid south. This means that even when we're dry, we can trust God to send regular blessings as common as each morning's dew on the ground to refresh and nourish us. Third, the Lord himself pours blessings on those He loves. Make no mistake, we're in enemy territory, and we're in a fight. The thing that blocks our fruitfulness most often is division—in families, on teams, in churches, and in denominations. Mount Zion became David's stronghold, the place where he ran for refuge and launched military expeditions with his faithful soldiers. In the same way, we experience God's anointing, His blessings, and His strength as we live and serve together in unity—and it's amazingly "good and pleasant." If we stay in solidarity with God and with each other, the gates of Hell will not prevail against us.

Who Are We?

Isn't it amazing? Who are we that God, the creator of heaven and earth, would draw us into the partnership of His own prayers through the Holy Spirit who searches the deep things of God? Who are we that He would reveal himself and His wisdom to us? How can it be that the God of the universe is our Father? As a loving Father, He has no favorites. He shares His heart and His mind with all those He loves. Jesus is the head of the body, and He gives part of His message to each of us so that none of us gets too cocky and we learn to depend on each other. When we come together to pray in the Spirit, with understanding, and in agreement, God is in the middle of us and amazing things will happen. Count on it.

Think about it:

1. Which point seems most applicable to you as you see yourself pastoring the process? How will you navigate it?

2. What is your next step? What do you need in order to take it?

3. What do you hope happens?

ACKNOWLEDGMENTS

I'm so thankful for my close friend, Pat Springle, for helping me create this book. Thank you for helping me get my words in print. You are the best! I mean that.

I'd also like to acknowledge all of the incredible biblical scholars who contributed to this work. Thank you, Dr. Paul Brooks, for the many hours and work you put into this project. Also, thank you, Dr. John Davidson, Dr. Chris Railey, Dr. Mark Batterson, Dr. Doug Oss, and Dr. Doug Witherup. All of you have been a great help.

I appreciate all of my pastor friends who gave me biblical and practical feedback on how P3 can be a useful tool in the local church. Thank you, Preston Ulmer, Wes Combs, Mark Brewer, Brian Galbraith, Hunter Wilson, Dan Hunter, Kelvin Co, and Andy Lehmann. You guys are amazing!

As always, I want to thank my wife and my best friend, Jenni. You are so good to me. I can't imagine doing life without you. I love you with all my heart.

Lastly, I want to thank my three sons, Dillon, Hunter, and Dakota. The three of you always have my back . . . and for that, I am forever grateful. I pray that my ceiling will always be your floor. And I can't forget my two new daughters-in-law, Emily and Holly. Thank you for making this Dad happy to finally have girls!

ABOUT THE AUTHOR

Scott Wilson is the Senior Pastor of Oaks Church, ministering to approximately 4,000 people every week in South Dallas area. He is a frequent conference speaker, and provides mentorship for hundreds of pastors and church leaders.

With more than 20 years of experience in full-time pastoral ministry, dozens of pastors and leaders have been strengthened to fulfill their destiny and dreams through Scott Wilson Consulting. The organization comes alongside church and marketplace leaders to enable them to achieve the full potential of what God has called them to do.

Because of Scott's desire to train the next generation, he created the Oaks School of Leadership, a specialized ministry training program providing young leaders with hands-on experience while earning college credits. Through this intense training program, hundreds of students have been educated, prepared for ministry and sent out as ministry leaders.

Scott has written several books, including his latest releases *Spread the Fire: Spirit Baptism in Today's Culture* and *Clear the Stage: Making Room for God*. Scott's previous titles include *The Next Level: A Message of Hope for Hard Times* (Baxter Press) and *Steering Through Chaos: Mapping a Clear Direction in the midst of transition and change* (Zondervan).

THE VIEW
FROM THE PEW

Paul Brooks, D.Min., Professor of Theology and Vice President for Academics at Southwestern Assemblies of God University

Many years ago when I was a young pastor, an elder sought to encourage me by saying, "Never forget the view from the pew." As you might imagine, it really didn't have anything to do with pews; it had everything to do with views. Pastors are often trying to get things done and seeking to motivate people toward greater involvement in the things of God. They share vision and hope to motivate others to pursue it. In a general sort of way, pastors are about leading and congregants are about following. My elder friend wanted to challenge me as a pastor-leader to always intentionally consider the other point of view. I knew ultimately this would involve leading by doing, not just by saying.

As a local church member, I have a preference to be part of a church where the Holy Spirit is actively and authentically engaged. To be sure, this isn't all I want, but it is very important to be where the Spirit's presence and voice are nurtured and experienced regularly. Thankfully, this is truer today than at any point previously in my life. Jesus spoke much of the Holy Spirit in His last great discourse (John 14-16). I want to be responsive to Jesus' guidance. One of His claims about the Holy Spirit is that "He will take you by the hand and guide you into all the truth there is. He won't draw attention to himself, but will make sense out of what is about to happen and, indeed, out of all that I have done and said. He will honor me; he will take from me and deliver it to you. Everything the Father has is also mine. That is why I've said, 'He takes from me and delivers to you.' (Jn.16. 12-15, MSG). Obviously, according to Jesus, the Holy Spirit is revealing and sharing.

I don't think the Spirit is trying to be silent. He's speaking to people who have ears to hear Him, and Jesus pointedly calls believers to develop their "hearing" (Rev. 2-3). The Spirit is not sent here by Jesus to hide things, but to reveal things. Paul called to mind the words of Isaiah about God's preparations for His people and went on to claim, ". . . to us God revealed them through the Spirit; for the Spirit searches all things, even the depths of God" (1 Cor. 2:10). Paul prayed in tongues a great deal (1 Cor. 14.18), and it meant so much to him. He knew this practice was good and necessary for the Church, and he clearly demanded, "Do not forbid to speak in tongues" (1 Cor. 14.39). Paul wrote that the Spirit knows the thoughts of God which "we have received . . . that we might know the things freely given to us by God" (1 Cor. 2.12). He taught the Galatians that God sent the Holy Spirit into our hearts, "crying, 'Abba! Father!'" (Gal. 4.6). Paul amplifies this kind of dynamic in Romans 8 when he admits that we don't know how to pray as we should, "but the Spirit Himself intercedes for us with groanings too deep for words" (Rom. 8.26). There is a reality called the "communion (participation, sharing) of the Holy Spirit" (2 Cor. 13.14). It is not without us, or in spite of us, or over top of us, but it is with us and through us that the Spirit prays forth the will of God (Rom. 8.27). So it's actually the Spirit in us who cries out to God about our relationship to Him, our identity in Him (Rom. 8.16), and His will and glorious purposes (Rom. 8.27-39). There's undeniably something pure and effective about praying in the Holy Spirit. It's praying that supersedes the intellect and sets aside carnal desires, ill will and misinformation.

Peter indicated that it was the revelation of the Spirit that informed the prophets concerning the Christ (1 Pet. 1.11). He went on to explain that no prophecy is simply a matter of human will but a partnership in which "men moved by the Holy Spirit spoke from God" (2 Pet. 1.21). Jesus indicated to the Pharisees that David spoke by the Spirit when he called Him "My Lord" in the Psalms (Mt. 22.42-45; Ps. 110.1). It is the Spirit who watches over the eternal revelation of Scripture and shines light upon it so that its truth would be mediated to our spirits. So, the Spirit speaks *to* God's people in all kinds of revelations and speaks *through* God's people in prayers, praises, abundant thanksgivings and prophetic utterances. Is it any wonder then that Paul would declare, "I will pray with the Spirit, and I will pray with the understanding" (1 Cor. 14.15)? His direction for those who speak in tongues is pray to interpret them (1 Cor. 14.13). It isn't about feeling good or becoming known, rather it's about knowing what God is doing. This then is how the gathered body is edified as people come into an understanding of the prayer/praise offered and can join in with their authentic "amen" to utterances in tongues (1 Cor. 14.16). Paul sought engagement with the Spirit and encouraged the church to the same as he challenged them three times to earnestly desire the manifestations of the Spirit (1 Cor. 12.31; 14.1, 39).

As the church embraces the biblical concepts summarized above, it will experience a rich fellowship in the Spirit (2 Cor.

13.14). Its prophetic utterances will be strengthening (1 Cor. 14.3), its prayers will be powerful and effective (Jas. 5.16), and its ministries will be emboldened and Christ glorifying (Acts 4.23-31).

The Church must be a praying Church. "Pray at all times in the Spirit," Paul commanded, as he encouraged persistence and prayerful concerns about a bold ministry of the gospel (Eph. 6.18-20). Praying with the Spirit (i.e., in spiritual languages inspired by the Spirit himself), praying with understanding (i.e., with an interpretation illumined by the inspiration of the Spirit), and praying in agreement (i.e., a deep conviction and joining to the mind of Christ) where the corporate family of Christ can collectively enter into an authentic unity of "amen" is a grand expression of God's plan for a praying church. One may call this process "P3" or any other useful expression. In the end, it's an engagement between the Holy Spirit and God's gathered people in pursuit of the purposes and heart of God.

Aside from the theology and the stories of how all this came to pass at the Oaks, two concepts stand out significantly to me in this book. One is the idea of participation. I grew up in a Pentecostal heritage in which I observed that a few people in the church operated in the Spirit. I lived through an era in my middle years where it seemed to become the domain of platform personalities to operate in the Spirit. The consequence of this was to quench the Spirit and turn congregants into spectators. But now, with P3, it appears that there is a significant experience of many people in the operations of the Spirit. I see a new openness to the Spirit. I see earnest desire. I see a new kind of faith that the Spirit is indeed speaking to and through His people. I see it in young people. I see it in the elderly. I see it in the church staff, and

I see it in the congregation. This would not be happening without a leadership who intentionally gives time and priority to it. All around are visions, promptings, illumined scriptures, prophetic utterances and words of wisdom that accompany mighty intercessions in the Spirit. The Scripture describes this: "When you assemble, each one has a psalm, has a teaching, has a revelation, has a tongue, has an interpretation . . . you can all prophesy one by one" (1 Cor. 14:26-31). The view from the pew is that Spirit-filled believers need to know that their participation is biblical, desired and helpful.

The second is the theme of pastoring the process. I think it's an error to believe if it's just left up to people in some general way that the Holy Spirit is going to just take over. That's not really His way. His way is partnership (2 Cor. 13.14). The term there is "koinonia" and speaks of intimacy and intentionally working together. Pastoring the process simply means to help it along; to model it, teach it, guide it, coach it, affirm it, gently correct when necessary, assess it in the light of Scripture, and do what I call "door opening." It isn't the experience of an average person to just come in and take over the room. Humble, genuine people tend to stand back a bit in group situations. They are generally deferential. They are more likely to be spectators than to step forward. They are uncomfortable about taking risks in front of others. For everyday people to engage, someone needs to help them know how and when to engage. For their sake, and for everyone's sake, someone needs to say, "This is good; let's do it! God is at work in us and with us!" It's up to the leader to encourage involvement and to indicate the rules and decorum of experiences in the Spirit when the people gather. This leadership shouldn't be pressure-filled or be heavily focused on performance or comparisons. It's just "door opening." Whether it's a large group or a small group, the pastor or group leader is really the one who opens the door. When the people step through that door and engage, the fellowship of the Spirit will be awesome and great edifications will issue from it. Things won't be perfect, nor are they expected to be, but it will be a growing experience moving into the deep things from God. The view from the pew is that Spirit-filled believers need leaders to clearly explain how to engage the Holy Spirit and then make room for this involvement.

P3: A BIBLICAL PERSPECTIVE

John Davidson, Ph.D., Director of the Alliance for AG Higher Education, Director of CMN Discovery & Development, AG National Office

As a Pentecostal, I must hold two of my foundational values in tension: first, the Bible is my ultimate rule for faith and practice (2 Timothy 3:16), and second, the Holy Spirit was sent by Jesus to live in and empower believers in an ever-deepening relationship with the Father and the Son (John 16:13-15). Some might say, "Where's the tension in those?" The tension is that sometimes the Holy Spirit works in ways I don't see clearly spelled out in Scripture. Now, to be clear, because the Bible is my rule for faith and practice, everything must ultimately be measured against it, even what I sense to be the work of the Spirit. I don't believe the Spirit will ever act in a way that's contradictory to God's Word.

As much as the Bible has to say about the Holy Spirit, I wish it said more. There are some aspects of the Holy Spirit's person and work that just aren't spelled out as specifically as I would like. Of course, as someone who believes the Bible to be the inspired Word of God, I also believe that the Bible contains exactly what God wanted to tell us through His Word. That is to say, if God would have wanted to be more specific, He could have and would have.

This doesn't mean, however, that the words of Scripture are the last words God wants to speak to us. Jesus' words in John 16 point clearly to the fact that God has more to say to His people. "Whatever he (Holy Spirit) hears he will speak, and he will declare to you the things that are to come. He will glorify me, for he will take what is mine and declare it to you." (John 16:13-14 ESV here and throughout). Just listen to all of that future-leaning language! The Holy Spirit will keep hearing, keep declaring, keep glorifying, keep taking what is the Son's and declaring it to His followers. If we take the inspired Word of God seriously, we have to come to terms with the fact that God wants to keep speaking to us through His Holy Spirit.

Once you accept that, the next obvious question is how exactly the Holy Spirit speaks to His people. This is often where controversy emerges between different streams of evangelicalism, and even between different streams of Pentecostalism. Does the Holy Spirit continue only to speak through the Scriptures, or does He also speak in other ways? And if He does continue to speak in other ways, how exactly do they work? Based on the entirety of Acts and Paul's letters, I believe the Holy Spirit continues to speak to God's people through the Scriptures and through other means of divine revelation such as tongues, interpretation and prophecy. In 1 Corinthians 12-14 Paul discusses the role of the Holy Spirit in the life of the church, and yet these are only three chapters on such a critical component of our faith. I wish the Bible was clearer on this, but I am committed to engaging the Holy Spirit fully with what knowledge I do have and trusting God where I don't have clarity.

Here are two areas surfaced by this book in which I, as an honest theologian, wish I had more clarity from the Bible:

1. Is tongues uni-directional or multi-directional?

First Corinthians 14:2 says "the person who speaks in tongues speaks not to men, but to God." It is the Holy Spirit empowering the believer (Acts 2:4), to pray out of his or her spirit (1 Cor 14:14) to God. First Corinthians 14 lists four categories of the content of tongues: mysteries (14:2), prayer (14:15), praise (14:15; also Acts 2:11), and thanksgiving (14:16-17). All of these are said *to God* in tongues.

If the public use of tongues mirrors the private use, the interpretation of these utterances would also be *to God*. Regardless of the language (heavenly or English) the substance of the communication would be uni-directional, always directed *to God*. This is challenging to me because, in my 40 years of being Pentecostal, I've heard very few interpretations that sounded like they were directed to God. Interpretations usually get interpreted as God speaking to the church, such as: "I'm going to give you peace," or "Don't be afraid," or some other instructional message. I see no biblical reason why interpretation should change the direction of the prayer.

As a Pentecostal, I don't feel we have grappled with this enough. I think it's often easier for us to keep doing what we've experienced than to ask if it matches what God's Word says. And in this case, I don't think an explicit biblical case can be made that interpretation of tongues is multi-directional (used as a method for people to speak to God as well as for God to speak to people). It appears from what Paul says in 1 Corinthians 14 that interpretation of tongues is how others can "listen in" on a Spirit-filled believer who is declaring the mysteries of, praying to, praising, and thanking God. By hearing and understanding the content of the tongues, those listening can say "Amen" (1 Cor 14:16), being encouraged and built up.

2. Is there a difference between the public and private use of tongues?

In 1 Corinthians 14, Paul is explaining the corporate use of spiritual gifts; in other words, how spiritual gifts are supposed to work when the people of God are gathered together. However, Pentecostals have often believed that corporate use of tongues differs from private use because of Paul's distinction in 1 Corinthians 14:18-19, when he appears to separate his speaking in tongues "more than all of you" (in private) with speaking "with my mind" (in the church). Paul writes at length in chapter 14 about how important it is that tongues be interpreted in the corporate environment, but he never mentions interpretation relative to an individual's personal prayer time. Paul does say, "The one who speaks in a tongue builds up himself" (1 Cor 14:4), which is perfectly appropriate as long as that person is by himself or herself. So, speaking in tongues without interpretation is beneficial and productive for the individual. Interpretation, it seems, is only necessary in corporate worship where insiders and outsiders both need to understand the words in order to be built up.

With that said, I began this response to Scott's book by saying two things: The Holy Spirit is still hearing from Jesus and communicating new things to His people, and sometimes the Holy Spirit works in ways I don't see clearly spelled out in Scripture. The process Scott refers to as P3 (praying in the Spirit, praying with understanding, and praying in agreement) fits into both of these categories. P3 comes from the heart of a pastor and a church who have a high commitment to hearing what the Holy Spirit is saying to the church. While the Bible does have something to say about how we hear from God, it isn't perfectly prescriptive about all the ways this happens. For instance, 1 Corinthians 14 does not explicitly define the P3 process. If it did, there wouldn't be a need for Scott to write a book explaining it, but I'm thankful that he has.

If the process still doesn't seem to make sense to you, or if you're struggling to see how it connects with Paul's instructions to the church in Corinth, maybe this will help. It's an outline of 1 Corinthians 14 that shows what Paul was saying about the role of tongues and interpretation in the life of the church.

If anyone speaks in a tongue, he speaks to God (14:2) …
In a language he doesn't understand (14:2) …
Which builds him up (14:4) …
And can, if understood, build up the church (14:5) …
And building up the church should be our goal (14:12) …
So we should pray for the power to interpret tongues
    (14:13) …
Because God desires both for our spirits to pray and our
    minds to understand it (14:14-15) …
Allowing outsiders to be built up as well (14:16-17) …
That's why speaking in words people can understand is the
    most important thing we can do in corporate worship
    (14:18-19) …
And God desires that everyone participate in it (14:26) …
In a way that is orderly and peaceful (14:27-33) …
And subject to the prayerful evaluation of others in the
    church (14:29).

When you see 1 Corinthians 14 in this way, it sounds a lot like the P3 process described in this book.

I'm thankful for the message of this book because the church must not just *be open to hear* from God; the church should *actively seek to hear* God's voice. Paul describes it as being "eager for manifestations of the Spirit" (1 Cor 14:12). This seeking and listening for the voice of God should take place in a community of believers who know that what they say and do should be measured against the rule of Scripture, and where other mature believers can judge and discern whether the interpretation, prophecy, or other manifestations of the Spirit are truly from God (1 Cor 14:29).

I'm also thankful for this book because it describes a spiritual process that I have lived. I received the baptism in the Holy Spirit as a teenager, but it wasn't until my 30s that I began asking God to show me what the Spirit of God was praying through my spirit. I was blown away as God began giving me words, pictures and ideas that I knew were not coming from my own imagination or creativity. When I shared this with other believers with whom I was praying, I would often find incredible alignment between what I was hearing from God and what they were hearing. In every case, our first response was to ask, "Does what we collectively heard from God glorify Jesus, have a basis in Scripture, and edify the church?" If it doesn't meet any one of those qualifications, we need to pray together again.

Do I see this P3 process exactly described in Scripture? No. Do I believe it is a valid application of the principles of Scripture? Yes. God desires to speak to His people, through His Spirit, confirmed by the believers, for their benefit. The process laid out in this book, when practiced eagerly and carefully within a loving group of believers, has the potential to unlock a new level of spiritual passion and sensitivity that the church today desperately needs.

NOW MORE
THAN EVER

By Chris Railey, D.Min., Senior Director, Center for Leadership and Church Development, Assemblies of God

"What difference does it make?" This question articulates the tension many feel concerning the theology and practice of the baptism in the Holy Spirit. To adequately pass on our Pentecostal faith and practice of the gifts of the Spirit to the next generation, this tension must be resolved, and therefore, this question must be answered. What difference does the baptism in the Holy Spirit, evidenced by speaking in other tongues, really make? Why don't more churches who believe this theologically practice it regularly? Why don't more churches who practice this regularly grow numerically? After all, isn't it in part a gift to enhance our witness of Christ to the world around us? Why don't more people who advocate for and operate in the power and gifts of the Spirit exhibit more fruit of the Spirit? Could it be that we have sound theology but poor execution? Maybe it would be helpful to better articulate and demonstrate to an emerging generation the difference the Holy Spirit actually makes individually in the life of the believer and corporately in the life of the church. The truth is, it makes a big difference.

I struggled to receive the baptism in the Holy Spirit in my own life and did not receive my prayer language until the age of twenty-six. I was raised in a Christian home with Pentecostal theology. In my formative years, I saw the weird and the healthy . . . and everything in between. I came to appreciate my Pentecostal heritage and always believed in the gifts and power of the Holy Spirit, that it is for today and available to every believer. There was, however, a certain fear factor I developed with the baptism in the Holy Spirit. I didn't understand it, I was afraid to go down to the front of the church (which was the only context I ever saw it as I grew up) and attempt to receive it, and I it was all so dramatic and intimidating that I tended to avoid it. I remember being thirteen years old praying at the altar on a Sunday night after the message, minding my own business, when a man accosted me by putting his hand on my forehead. With the scariest face and the most intimidating voice, he said, "Do you want to receive the baptism in the Holy Ghost?"

Terrified, I said "NO" and went back to my seat! That began a thirteen-year journey to receive my prayer language, marked first by fear, followed by a deepening curiosity, and finally a desperate desire to receive all God had for me. As a twenty-six-year-old seminary student, I was hungry to receive the baptism in the Holy Spirit, and at the same altar where I'd prayed thirteen years earlier, I again on a Sunday night went forward to pray, this time full of desire and anticipation to receive the Holy Spirit. I prayed for an hour and a half that night, people gathered around me reciting every Pentecostal cliché you can imagine to get me to receive. I stood, I knelt, I wept, and I cried out . . . and still, nothing happened. It was my worst fear come true. Looking back, I can see how God needed to purge me that night, not of any specific sin, but of my pride and need for control. I needed to be emptied before I could be filled. I was devastated that night and confided in my father about my disappointment and confusion. I'll never forget what he told me: "Son, don't make it about the gift or about tongues. Focus on the Giver . . . it's all about Jesus."

Three months later I was back at that same altar praying once again after a Sunday night service. The message was about being humble and hungry for more of God. I was the first one at the altar, people gathered around and the clichés came rolling in. Thirty minutes passed . . . and nothing happened. It seemed like a repeat of before. But this time, I remembered what my father had told me. I ignored all the people around me and began to just worship Jesus. I said the Name of Jesus over and over and became overwhelmed with joy as I worshipped, and in almost an anti-climactic way, I began to speak in a heavenly language and was filled with the Holy Spirit!

The baptism in the Holy Spirit makes a difference in the lives of individuals. Yes, it gives you a greater ability to be an effective witness, but it also gives you a greater capacity to know, love and have intimacy with Jesus. I learned that it always has been and always will be all about Jesus! As my confidence grew, my communication with God was enhanced, the passion I felt on the inside began to find expression on the outside, and leadership gifts were uncovered—in short, the power of the Holy Spirit in my life made *all* the difference!

When I was exposed to Pastor Scott and how P3 began to function at Oaks Church, I saw the corporate difference it could make. In the past, corporate expressions of Spirit baptism and the gifts in operation were always limited to the same few people who gave public utterances in tongues, followed by a King James interpretation by the same few. We celebrated it as beautiful, but in reality it seemed mundane—and nothing and no one seemed to really change. P3 is different; it has moved my understanding beyond just the Spirit operating in worship settings to staff meetings and board rooms and any setting two or more are gathered. I've seen it affect decision making, meeting agendas, and the overall direction of the local church. As Pastor Scott describes in the book, it's one thing to come to a meeting with an agenda, but it's another to allow the Holy Spirit to set the agenda. I've personally experienced the difference it makes when high level leaders begin a meeting, not end a meeting, praying in the Spirit, with understanding, and in agreement. The wisdom, discernment and empowerment that comes from leading in this way makes *all* the difference in the life of the local church!

Let me go back to my opening questions: What difference does it make? How can we be Pentecostal without being weird? How can we pass our Pentecostal faith and practice to the emerging generation? P3 gives us a pathway and a roadmap to do just that. This process enables us to regularly see the difference it makes both individually and corporately. The stakes are too high in this age to do what we've always done and expect different results . . . and to lean on our own strength and understanding. We need the power, gifts, and fruit of the Holy Spirit in our lives and leadership now more than ever.

P3 PROPHETIC PRAYER MODEL

The P3 Prophetic Prayer Model is a powerful tool to guide you as you pray for someone at the altar. Following these steps does not have to be rigid, but you should work to gain proficiency in them so that praying prophetically becomes natural.

Step 1: Pray in the Spirit (Ephesians 6:18)

Step 2: Pray with Understanding (1 Corinthians 14:13-15)

Step 3: Pray in Agreement (1 Peter 4:11)

Guidelines for Speaking Prophetically

- Remember Paul's admonition that love supersedes all ministry (1 Corinthians 13:1-3). A person should feel the overwhelming love of the Father when they walk away from receiving ministry.

- Prophecy should strengthen, encourage, and comfort (1 Corinthians 14:3). The Sunday morning altar ministry is not the place to rebuke, admonish, correct, or scold.

- Criticism and anger are not signs of a prophetic calling, but rather, a wounded heart. The real prophetic gift is not simply seeing what is wrong in a person's life, but seeing how to build them up. Prophecy should build someone up; it does not tear a person down.

- All prophecy must be in line with the Bible.

- Do not add to what God gives you; simply share what you have been given. Sometimes the most powerful words seem silly or unimportant to us.

- Do not try to make the prophetic word apply to their life. Allow the Holy Spirit to make the application.

- Be careful not to project what God is doing in your own life.

- Sometimes the Lord communicates to us through our own feelings. If you suddenly feel frustrated, distracted, afraid, proud, etc., consider that the Holy Spirit may be giving you a clue to pray for that person. If you suddenly feel a sharp physical pain or sensation, it may be an indication that God is revealing to you an area to pray for healing.

- If you have a prophetic word regarding a specific date, marriage, birth, etc., DO NOT give it without first clearing it with a pastor.

RESOURCES

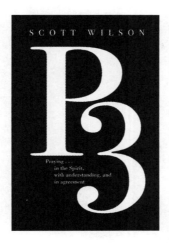

Visit **oaksresources.com** for information and resources such as a video of Pastor Scott speaking about P3, podcasts, books, sermon notes, the message library, and other helpful tools.

In addition, this site has a link to "Oaks Playbook: How we do what we do," which provides insights and ideas about how Pastor Scott leads Oaks Church.

To find his other books, go to these websites:

Steering through Chaos: Mapping a Clear Direction for Your Church in the Midst of Transition and Change (Amazon.com)

Ready, Set, Grow: Three Conversations that Will Bring Lasting Change to Your Church (Amazon.com)

The Next Level: A Message of Hope for Hard Times (Amazon.com)

Spread the Fire: Spirit Baptism in Today's Culture (MyHealthyChurch.com)

Clear the Stage: Making Room for God (MyHealthyChurch.com)